IMPERFECT
A STORY OF BODY IMAGE

Written by **DOUNYA AWADA**

Art by **MIRALTI FIRMANSYAH**

Colors by **FAHRIZA KAMAPUTRA**

Lettering by **TYLER SMITH**
for Comicraft

Zuiker
Press

Los Angeles

IMPERFECT: A STORY OF BODY IMAGE

Written by Anthony E. Zuiker
Art by Miralti Firmansyah
Cover art by Garry Leach
Colors by Fahriza Kamaputra
Lettering by Tyler Smith for Comicraft
Designed by Roberta Melzl
Edited by Dave Elliott

Founders: Michelle & Anthony E. Zuiker
Publisher: David Wilk

Published by Zuiker Press
16255 Ventura Blvd.
Suite #900
Encino, CA 91436
United States of America

Visit us online at www.zuikerpress.com

ISBN 978-1-947378-07-0 (hardcover)

PRINTED IN CANADA
April 2019
10 9 8 7 6 5 4 3 2 1

DEDICATED TO ... every young person who needs to be reminded they are not alone.

HOPE lies within these pages.

ZUIKER PRESS

... is a husband and wife publishing company that champions the voices of young authors. We are an **ISSUE-BASED** literary house. All of our authors have elected to tell their personal stories and be ambassadors of their cause. Their goal, as is ours, is that young people will learn from their pain and heroics and find **HOPE**, **CHANGE**, and **HAPPINESS** in their own lives.

TEACHER'S CORNER

SHANNON LIVELY

is a National Board Certified educator with a bachelor's degree in elementary education from the University of Nevada, Las Vegas, a master's degree from Southern Utah University, as well as advanced degrees in differentiated instruction and technology. In 2013, she was awarded the Barrick Gold One Classroom at a Time grant, and then chosen as Teacher of the Year. She is currently teaching fifth grade at John C. Vanderburg Elementary School in Henderson, Nevada.

WHY WE HONOR TEACHERS

We understand the amount of hard work, time and preparation it takes to be a teacher! At Zuiker Press, we have done the preparation for you. With each book we publish, we have created printable resources for you and your students. Our differentiated reading guides, vocabulary activities, writing prompts, extension activities, assessments, and answer keys are all available in one convenient location. Visit Zuikerpress.com, click on the For Educators tab, and access the **DOWNLOADABLE GUIDES** for teachers. These PDFs include everything you need to print and go! Each lesson is designed to cover Common Core standards for many subjects across the curriculum. We hope these resources help teachers utilize each story to the fullest extent!

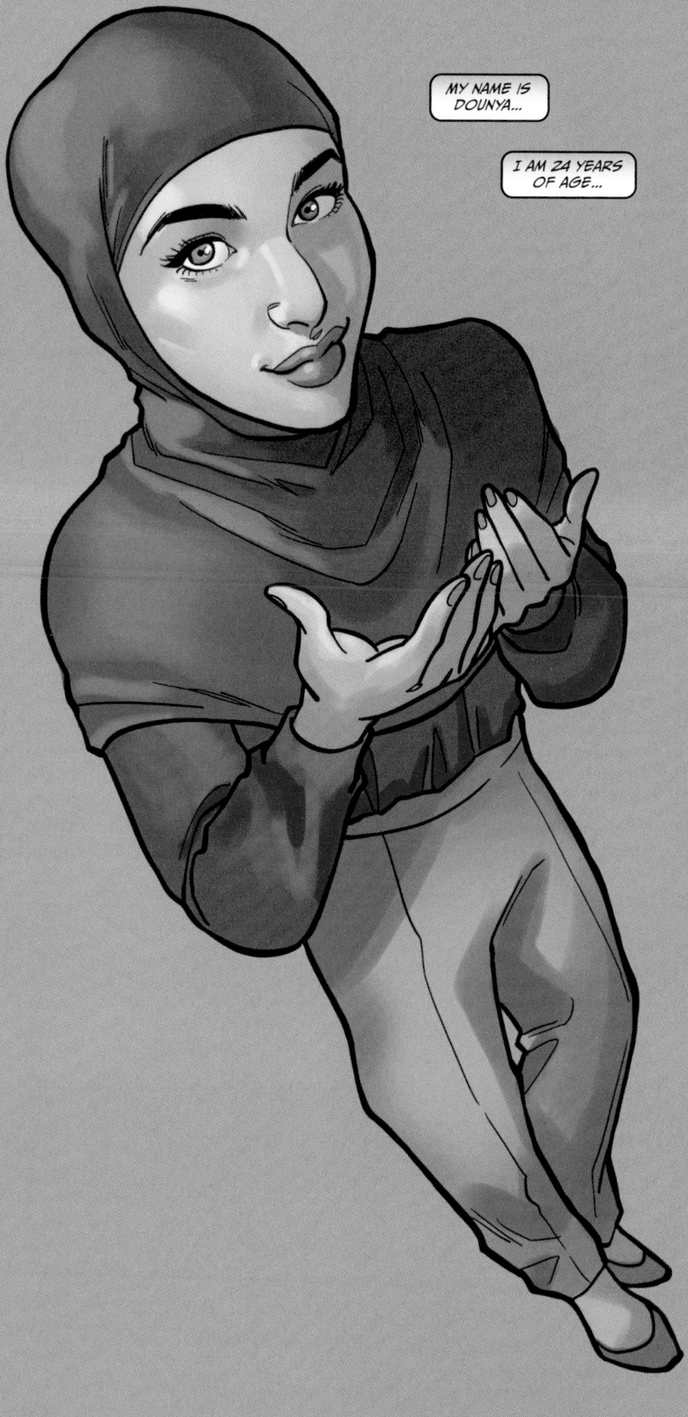
MY NAME IS DOUNYA...
I AM 24 YEARS OF AGE...

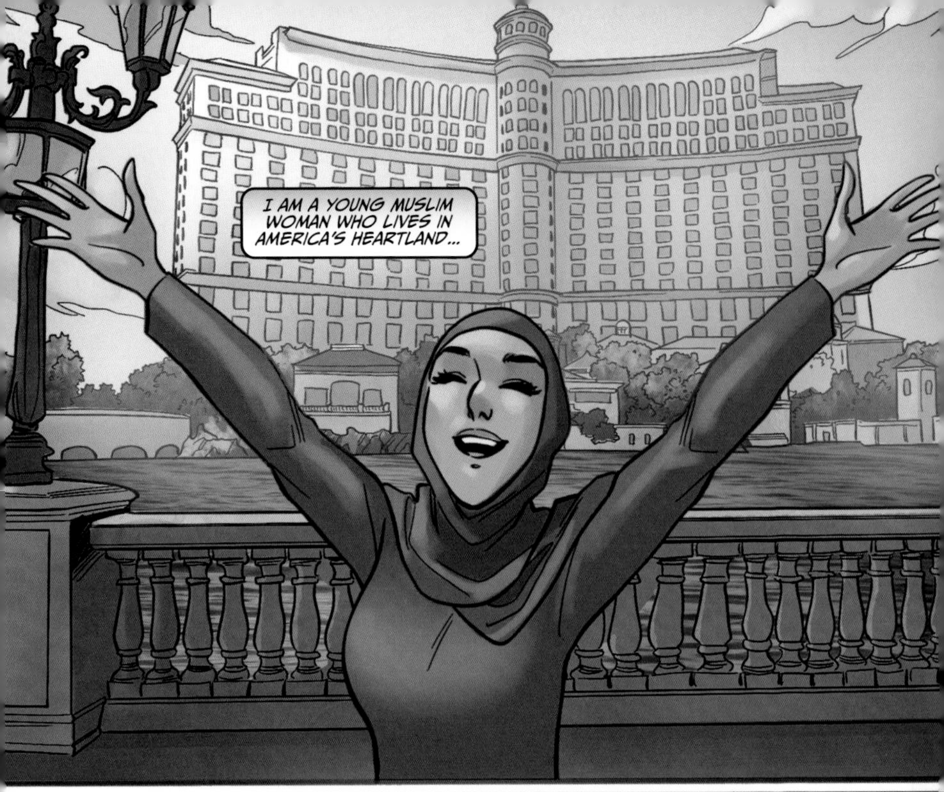
I AM A YOUNG MUSLIM WOMAN WHO LIVES IN AMERICA'S HEARTLAND...

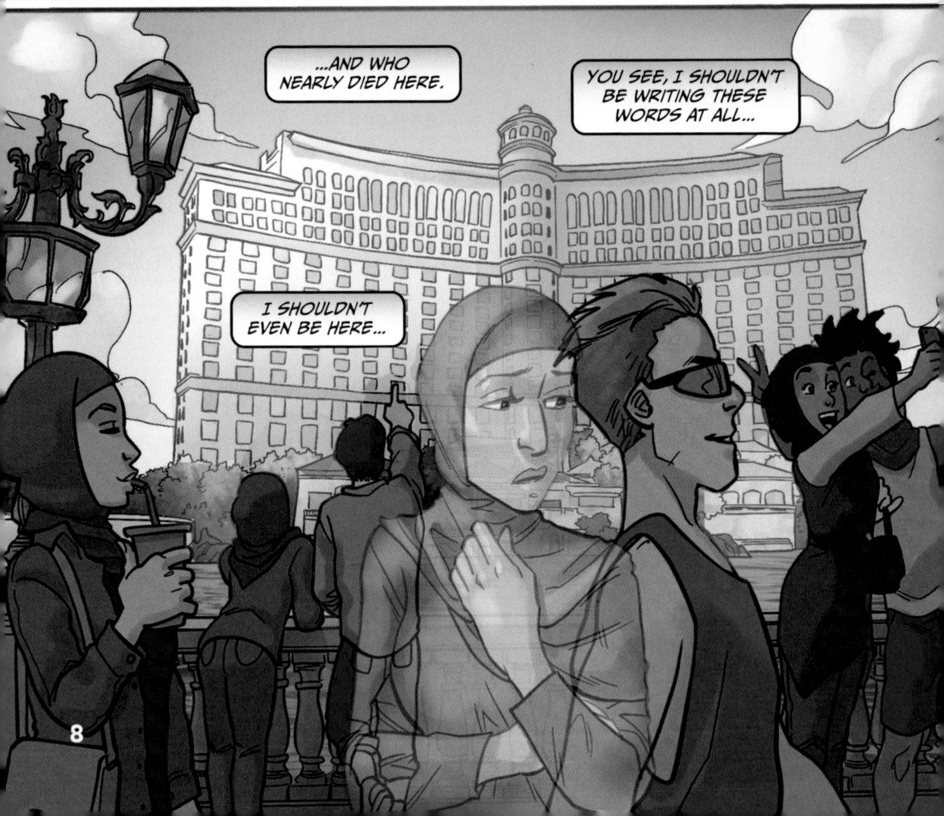
...AND WHO NEARLY DIED HERE.
YOU SEE, I SHOULDN'T BE WRITING THESE WORDS AT ALL...
I SHOULDN'T EVEN BE HERE...

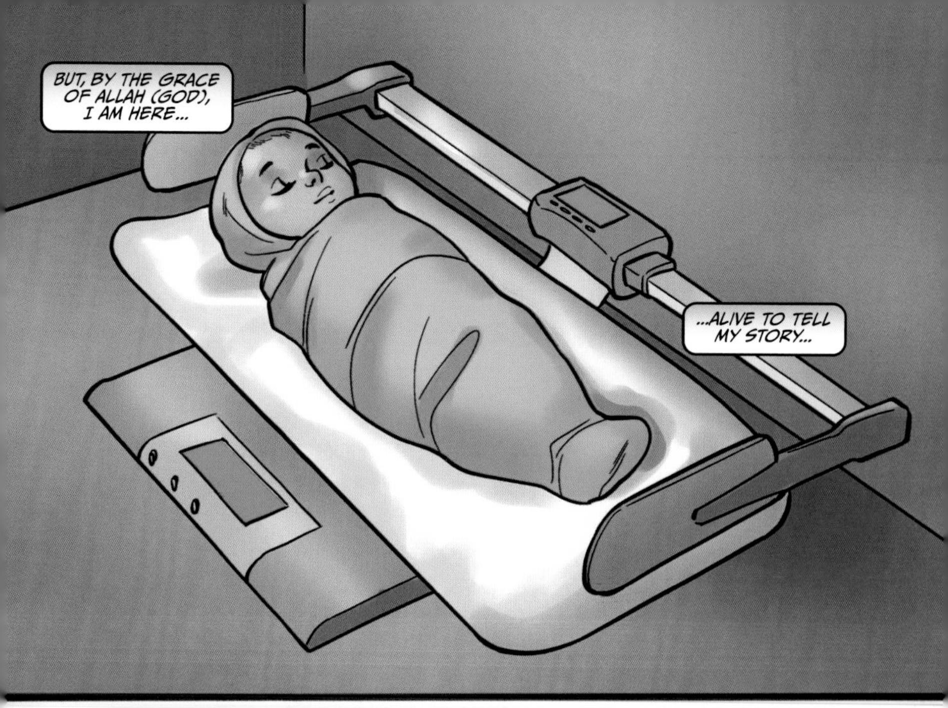
BUT, BY THE GRACE OF ALLAH (GOD), I AM HERE...
...ALIVE TO TELL MY STORY...

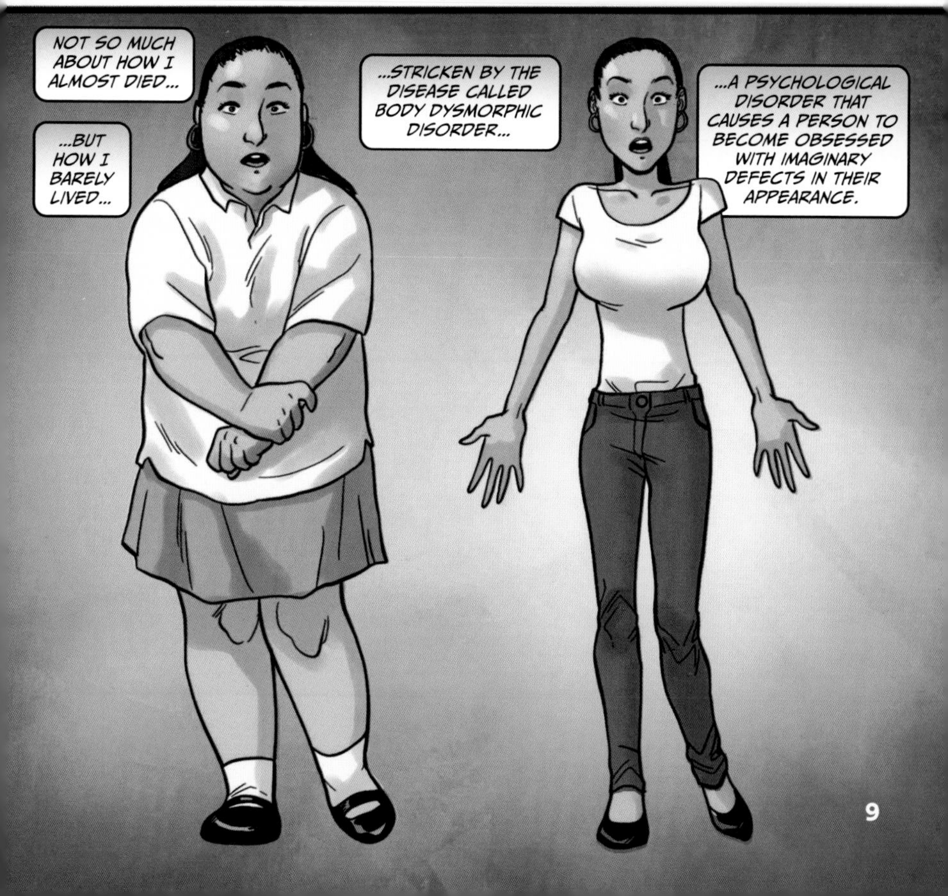
NOT SO MUCH ABOUT HOW I ALMOST DIED...
...BUT HOW I BARELY LIVED...
...STRICKEN BY THE DISEASE CALLED BODY DYSMORPHIC DISORDER...
...A PSYCHOLOGICAL DISORDER THAT CAUSES A PERSON TO BECOME OBSESSED WITH IMAGINARY DEFECTS IN THEIR APPEARANCE.

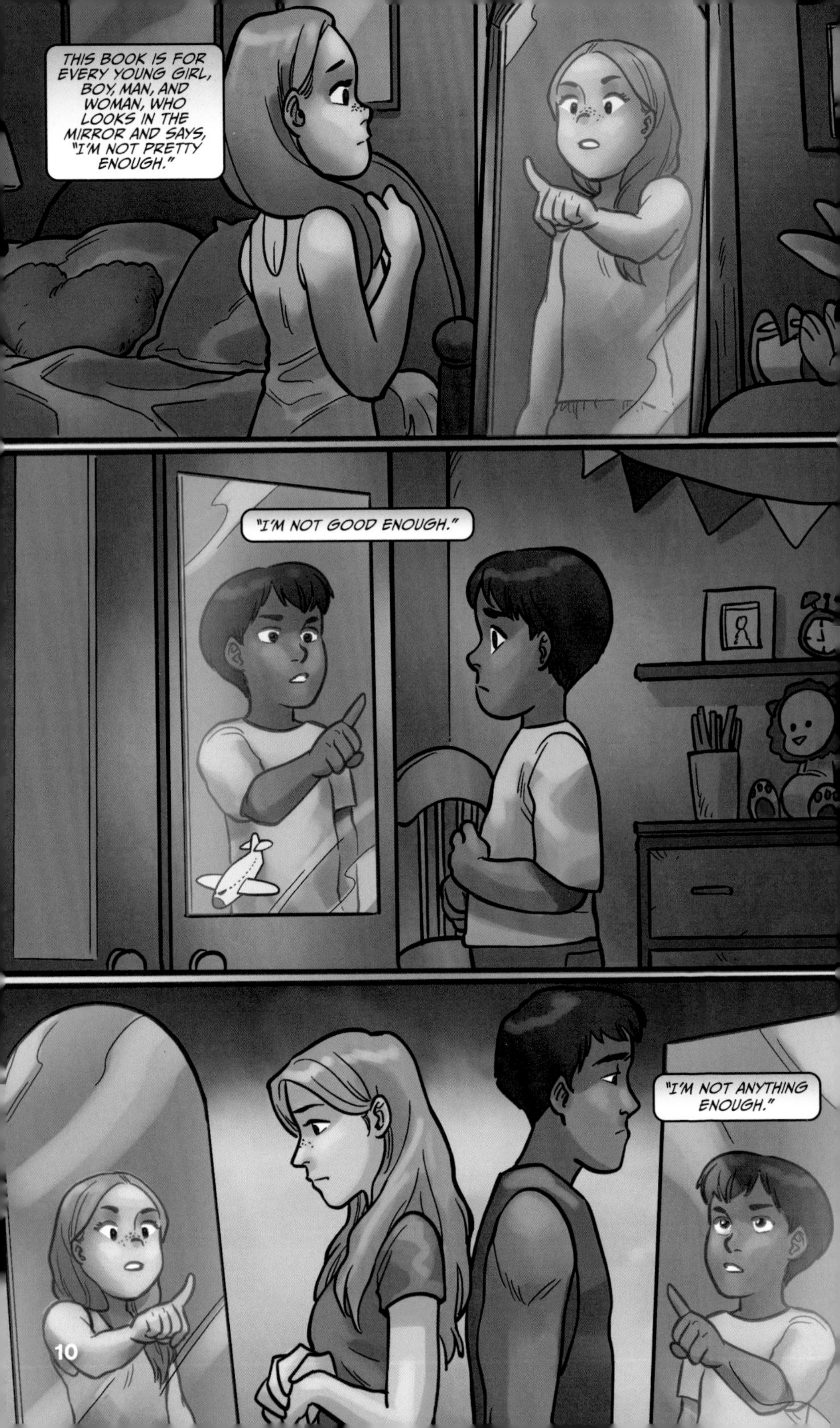
THIS BOOK IS FOR EVERY YOUNG GIRL, BOY, MAN, AND WOMAN, WHO LOOKS IN THE MIRROR AND SAYS, "I'M NOT PRETTY ENOUGH."
"I'M NOT GOOD ENOUGH."
"I'M NOT ANYTHING ENOUGH."

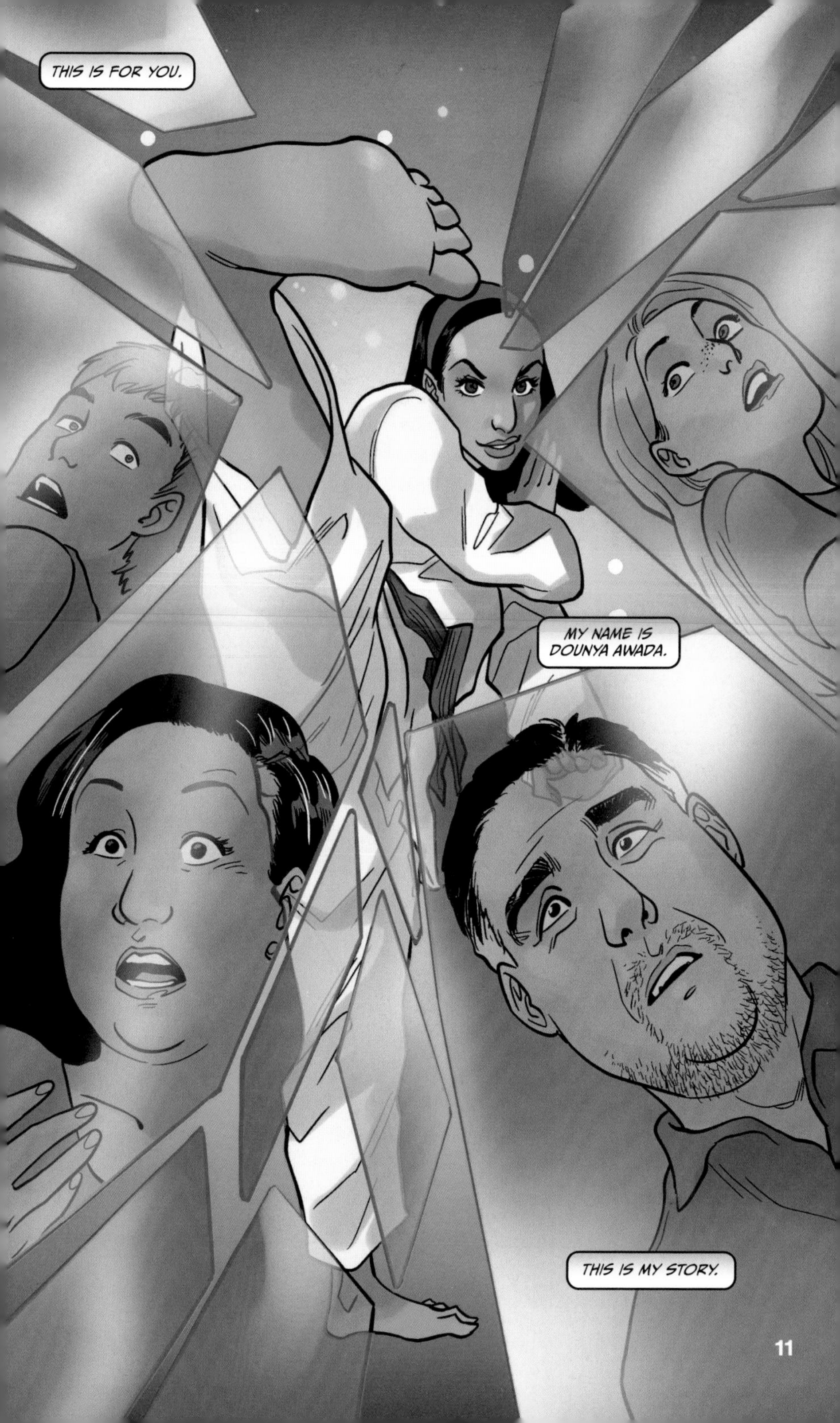
THIS IS FOR YOU.
MY NAME IS DOUNYA AWADA.
THIS IS MY STORY.

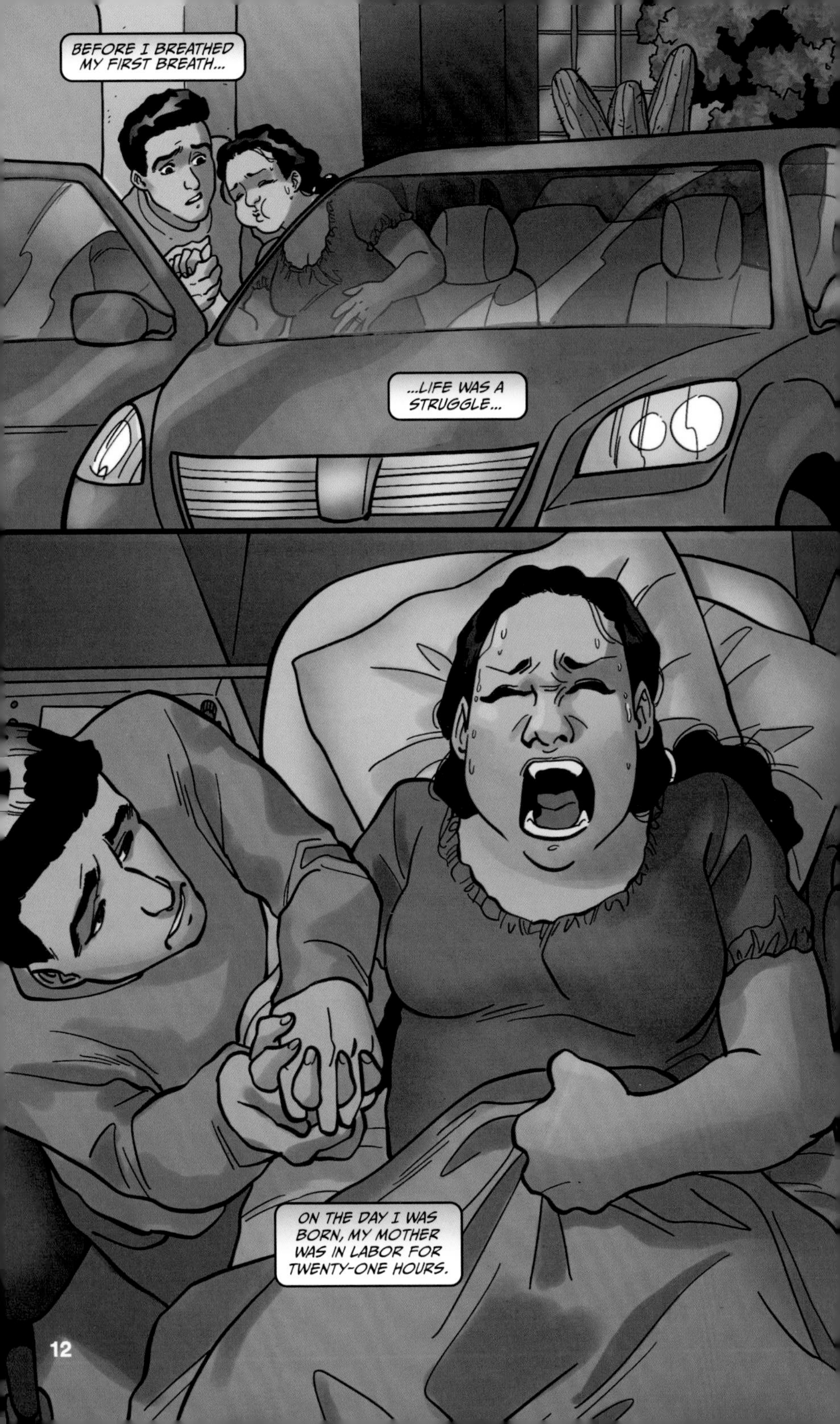
BEFORE I BREATHED MY FIRST BREATH...
...LIFE WAS A STRUGGLE...
ON THE DAY I WAS BORN, MY MOTHER WAS IN LABOR FOR TWENTY-ONE HOURS.

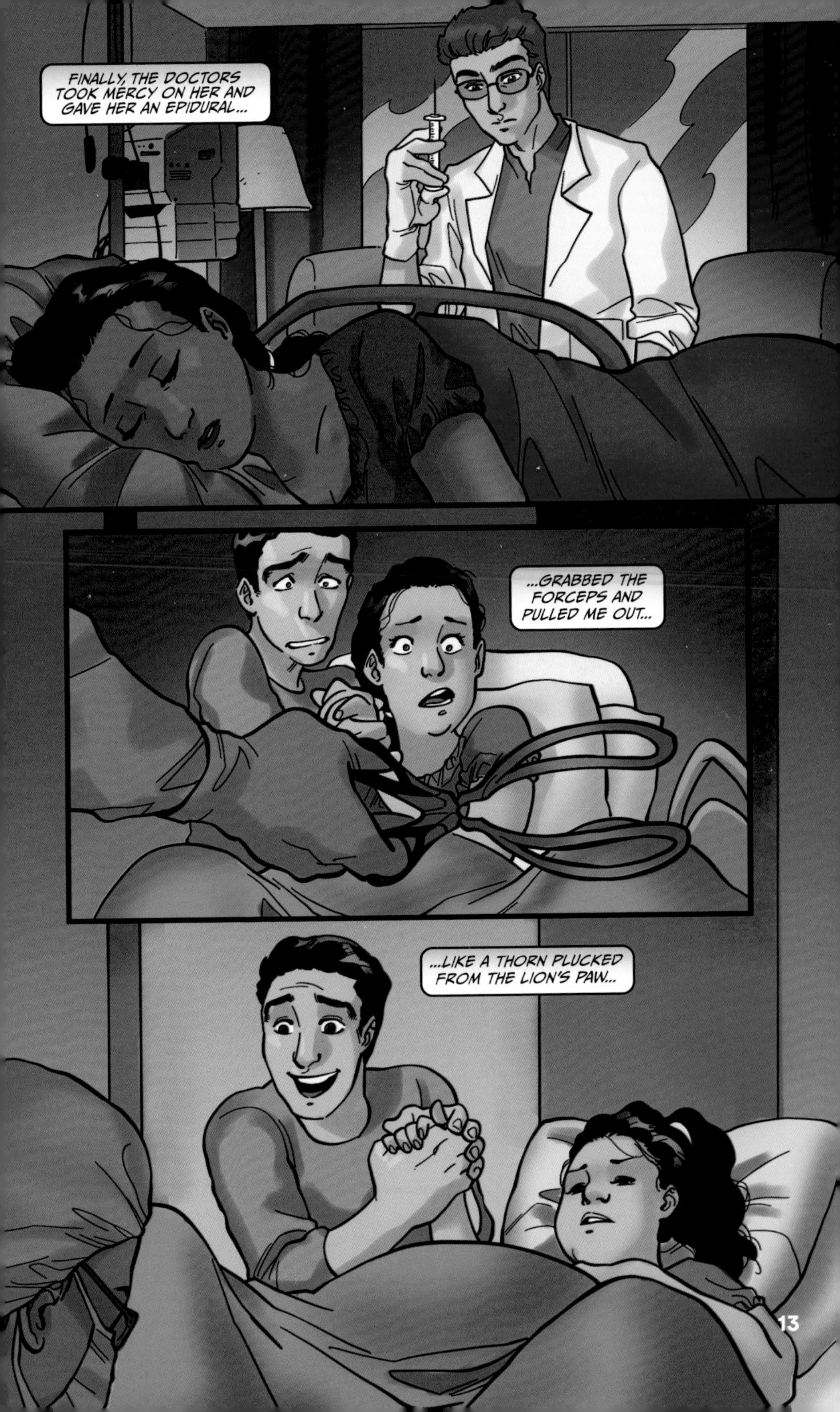
FINALLY, THE DOCTORS TOOK MERCY ON HER AND GAVE HER AN EPIDURAL...
...GRABBED THE FORCEPS AND PULLED ME OUT...
...LIKE A THORN PLUCKED FROM THE LION'S PAW...

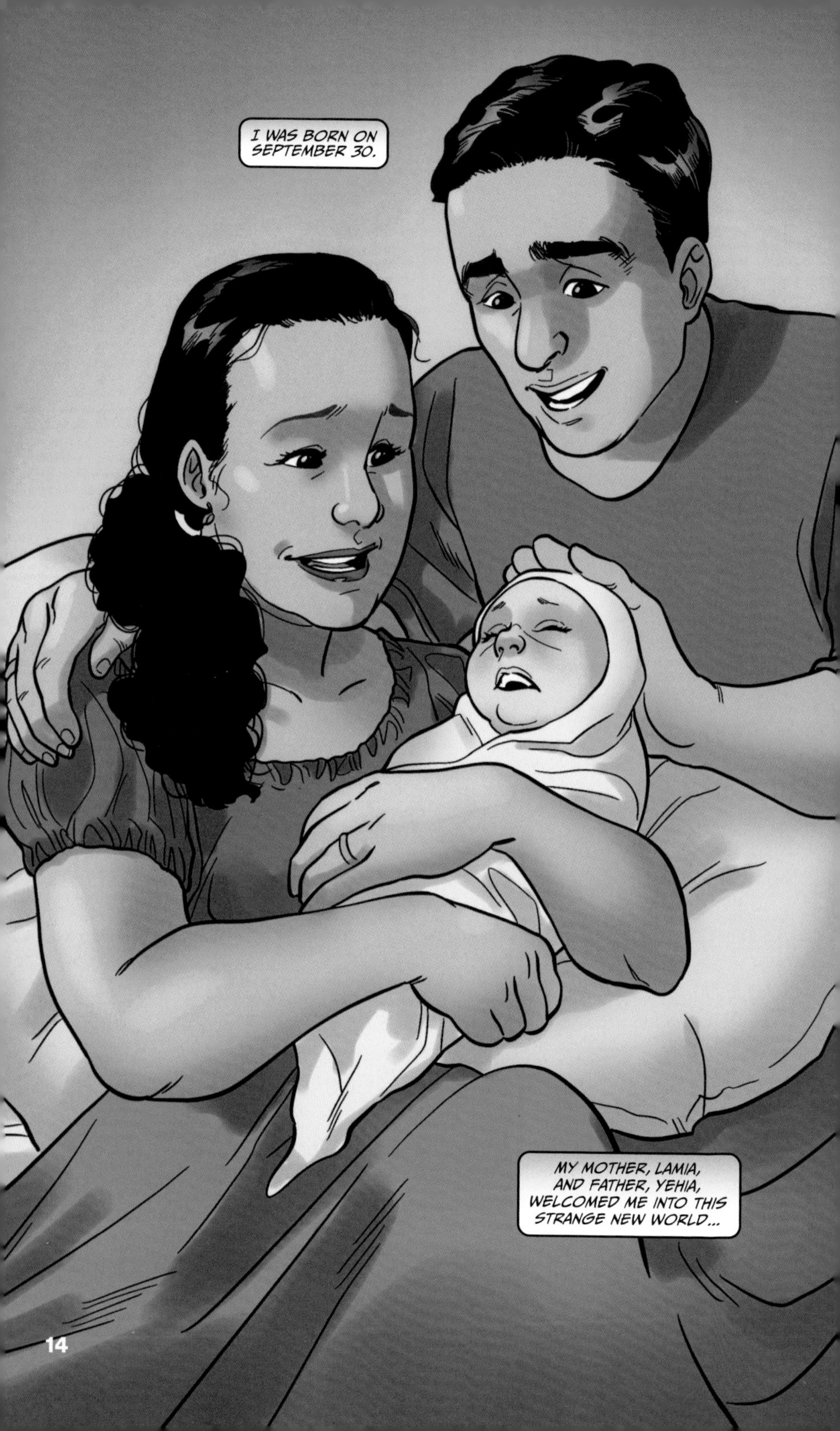
I WAS BORN ON SEPTEMBER 30.
MY MOTHER, LAMIA, AND FATHER, YEHIA, WELCOMED ME INTO THIS STRANGE NEW WORLD...

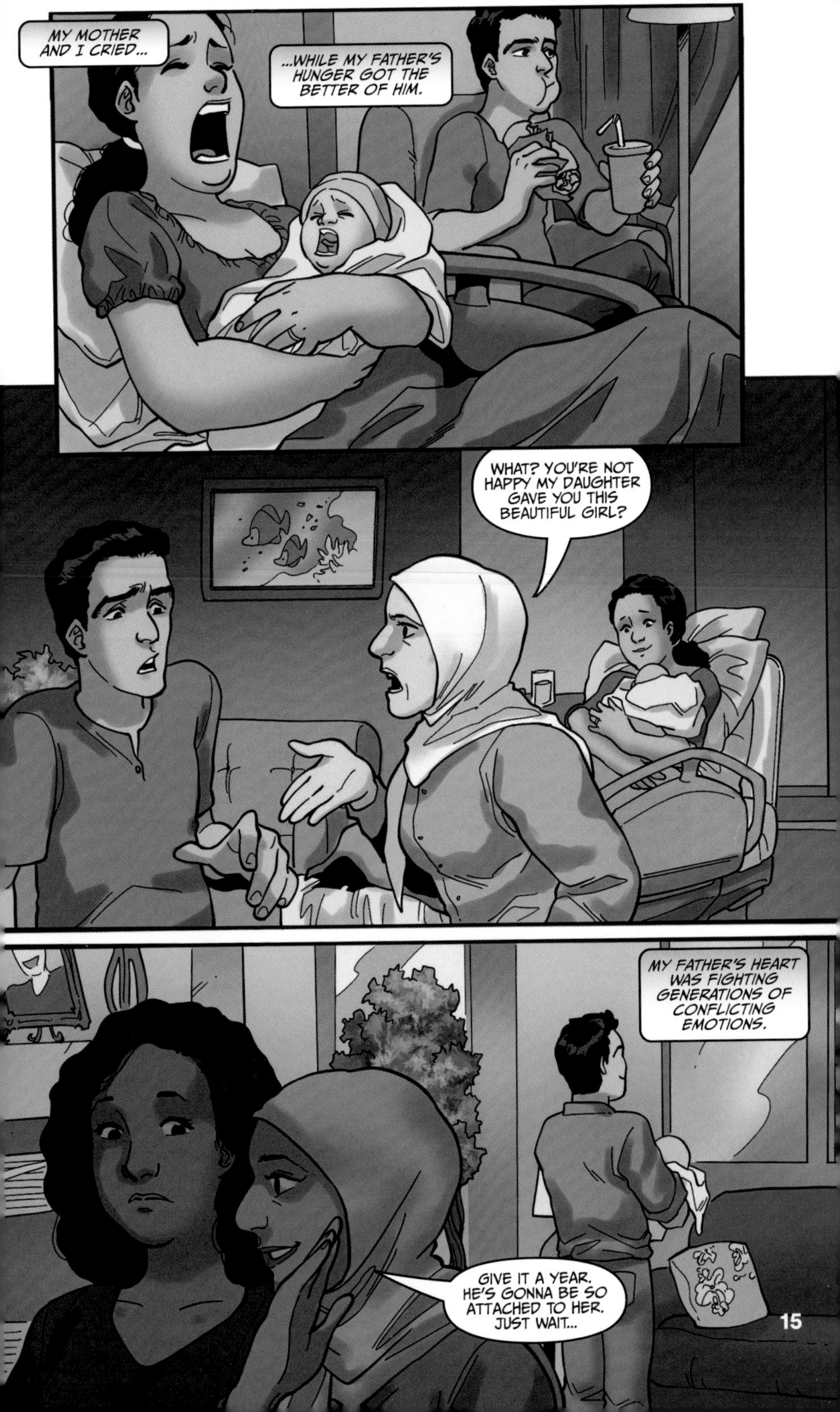

MY MOTHER AND I CRIED...
...WHILE MY FATHER'S HUNGER GOT THE BETTER OF HIM.
WHAT? YOU'RE NOT HAPPY MY DAUGHTER GAVE YOU THIS BEAUTIFUL GIRL?
MY FATHER'S HEART WAS FIGHTING GENERATIONS OF CONFLICTING EMOTIONS.
GIVE IT A YEAR. HE'S GONNA BE SO ATTACHED TO HER. JUST WAIT...

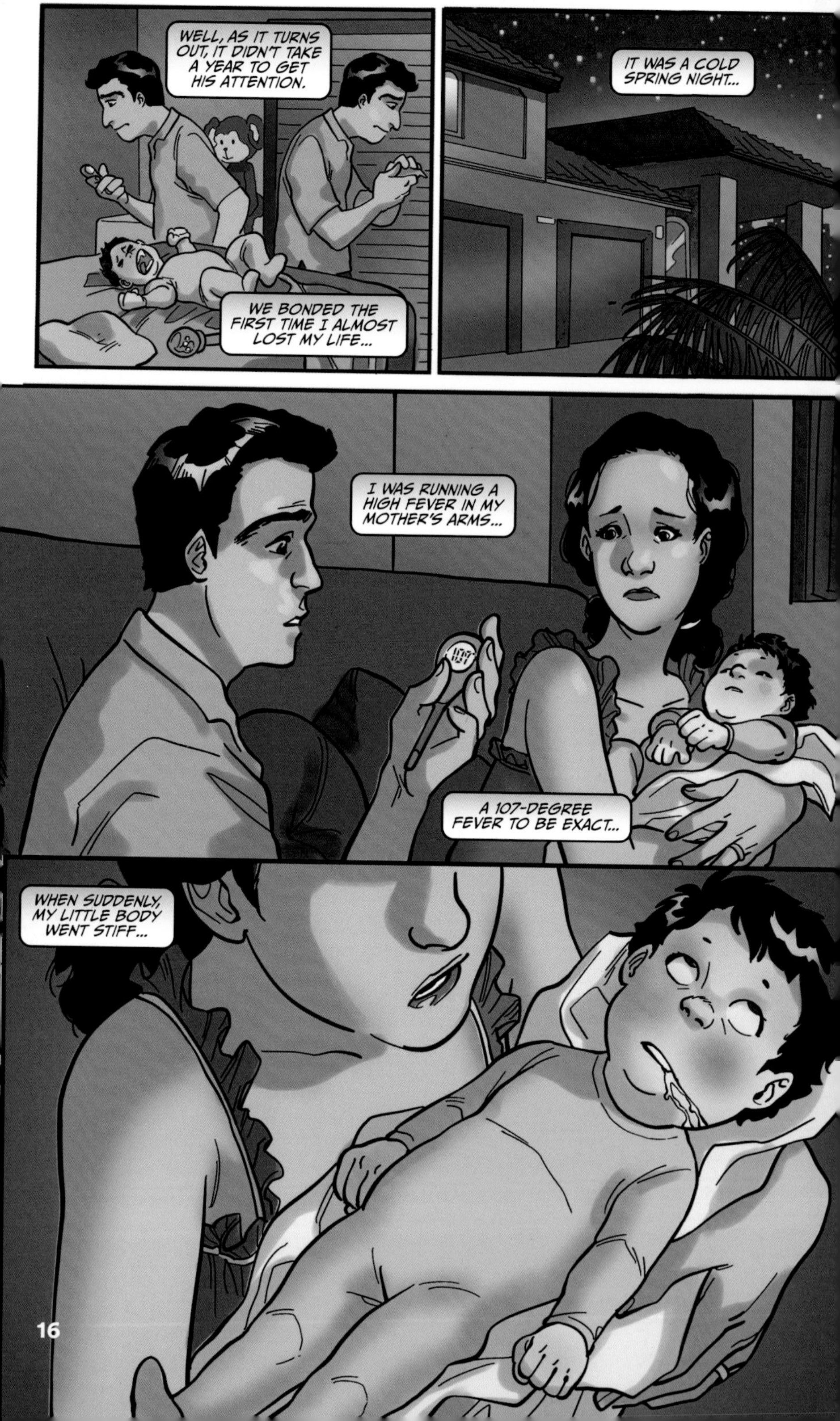

WELL, AS IT TURNS OUT, IT DIDN'T TAKE A YEAR TO GET HIS ATTENTION.
WE BONDED THE FIRST TIME I ALMOST LOST MY LIFE...
IT WAS A COLD SPRING NIGHT...
I WAS RUNNING A HIGH FEVER IN MY MOTHER'S ARMS...
A 107-DEGREE FEVER TO BE EXACT...
WHEN SUDDENLY, MY LITTLE BODY WENT STIFF...

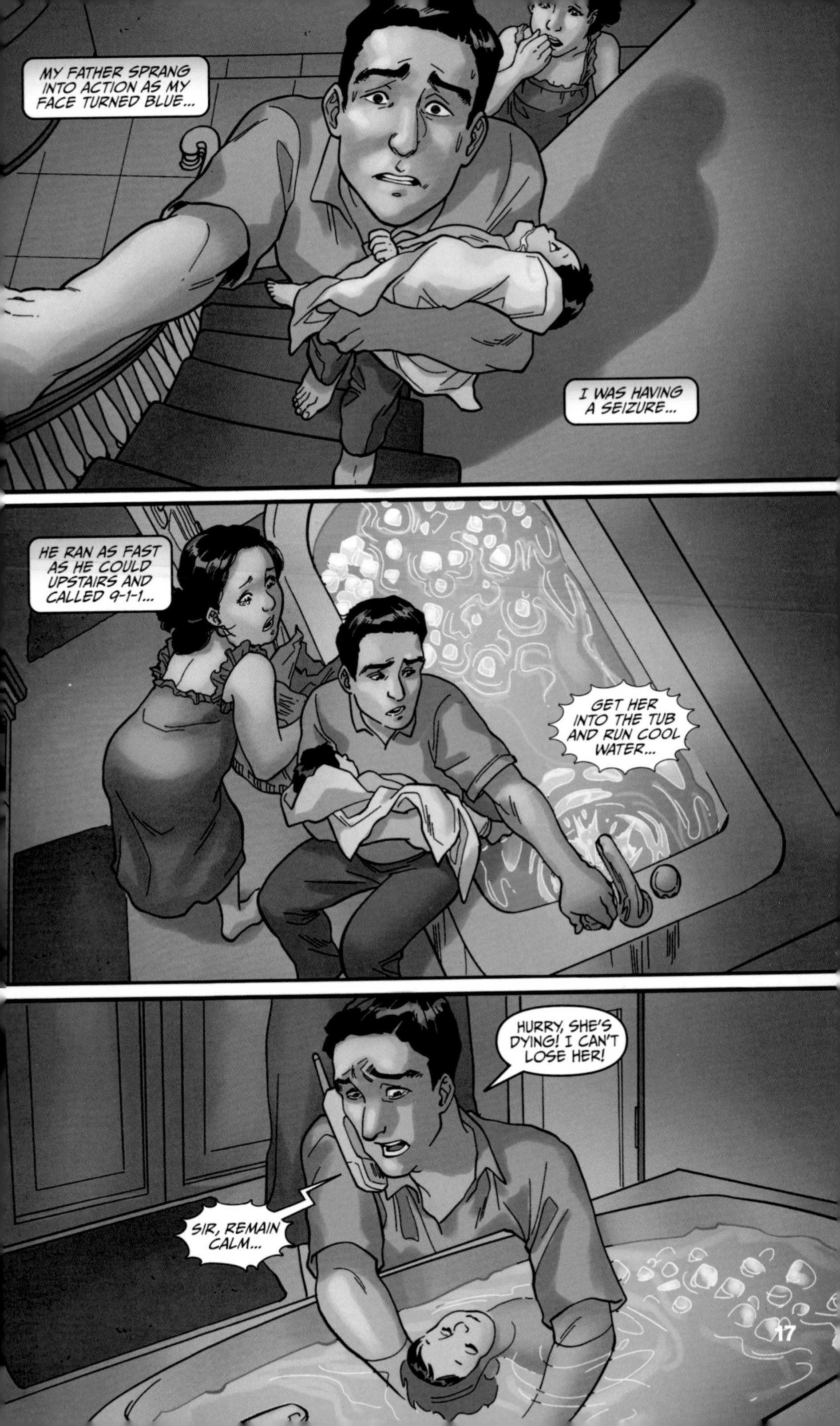

MY FATHER SPRANG INTO ACTION AS MY FACE TURNED BLUE...
I WAS HAVING A SEIZURE...
HE RAN AS FAST AS HE COULD UPSTAIRS AND CALLED 9-1-1...
GET HER INTO THE TUB AND RUN COOL WATER...
HURRY, SHE'S DYING! I CAN'T LOSE HER!
SIR, REMAIN CALM...

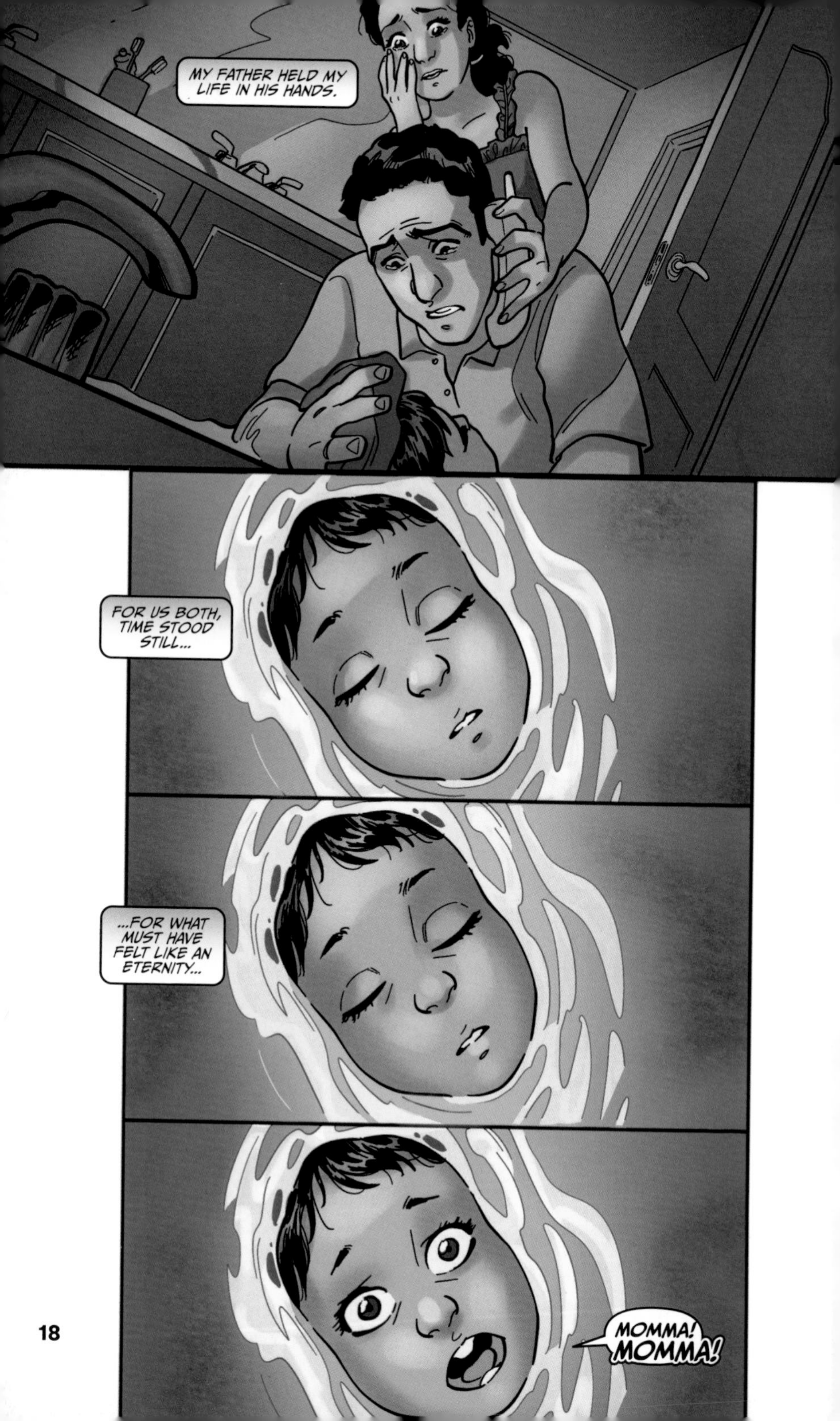

MY FATHER HELD MY LIFE IN HIS HANDS.
FOR US BOTH, TIME STOOD STILL...
...FOR WHAT MUST HAVE FELT LIKE AN ETERNITY...
MOMMA! MOMMA!

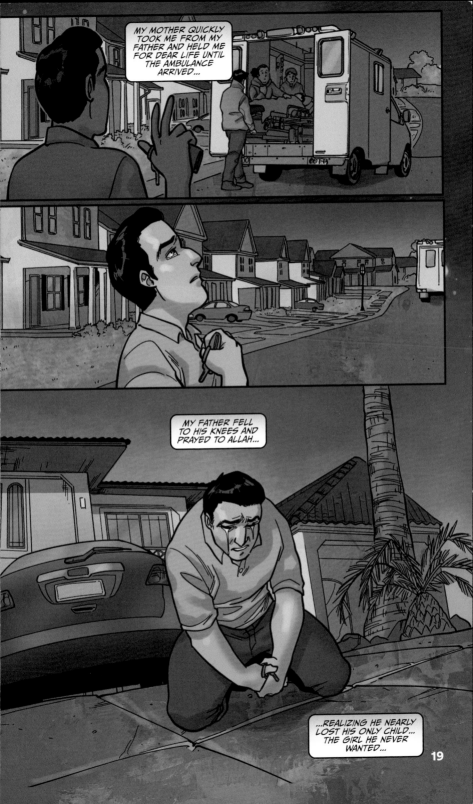

MY MOTHER QUICKLY TOOK ME FROM MY FATHER AND HELD ME FOR DEAR LIFE UNTIL THE AMBULANCE ARRIVED...

MY FATHER FELL TO HIS KNEES AND PRAYED TO ALLAH...

...REALIZING HE NEARLY LOST HIS ONLY CHILD... THE GIRL HE NEVER WANTED...

19

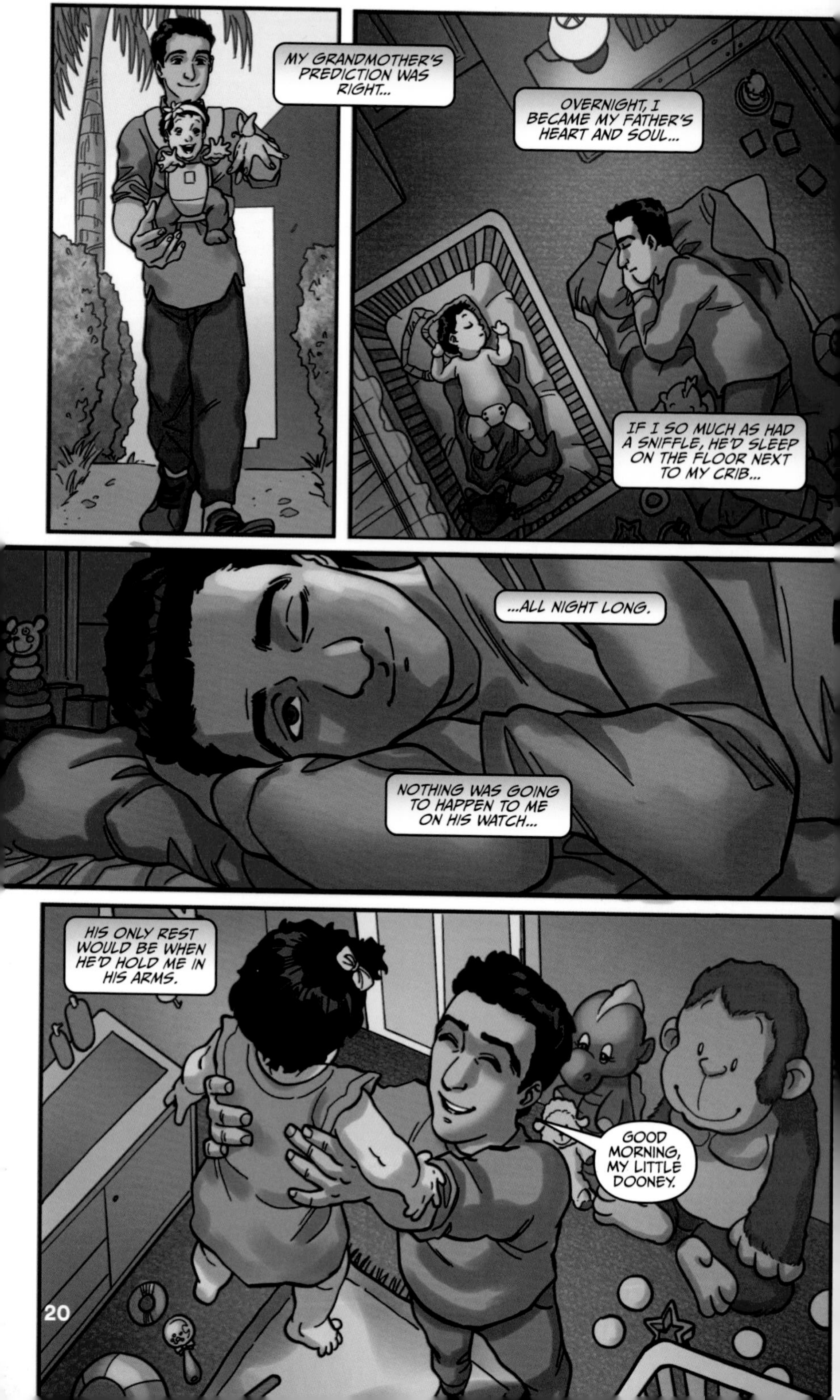
MY GRANDMOTHER'S PREDICTION WAS RIGHT...
OVERNIGHT, I BECAME MY FATHER'S HEART AND SOUL...
IF I SO MUCH AS HAD A SNIFFLE, HE'D SLEEP ON THE FLOOR NEXT TO MY CRIB...
...ALL NIGHT LONG.
NOTHING WAS GOING TO HAPPEN TO ME ON HIS WATCH...
HIS ONLY REST WOULD BE WHEN HE'D HOLD ME IN HIS ARMS.
GOOD MORNING, MY LITTLE DOONEY.

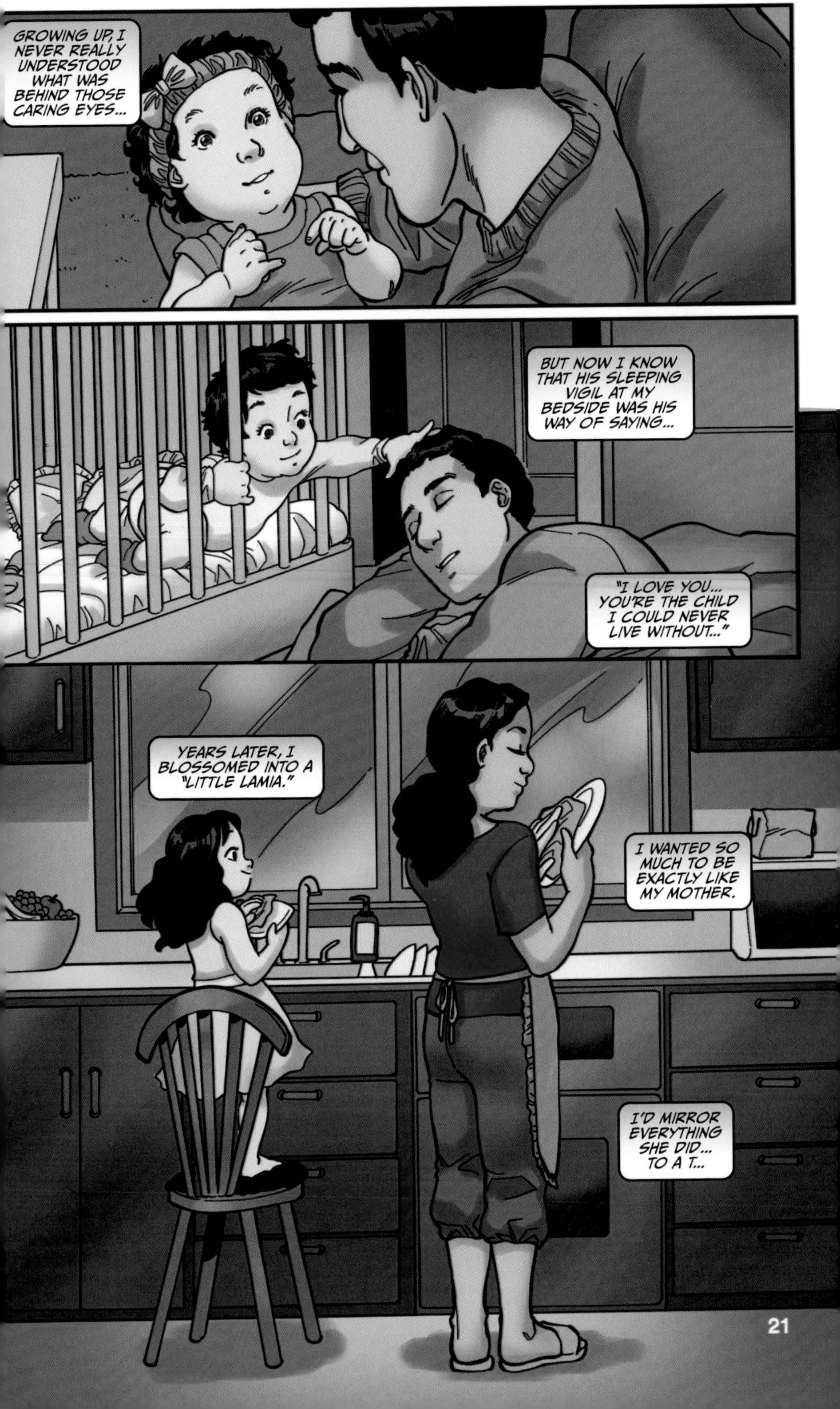
GROWING UP, I NEVER REALLY UNDERSTOOD WHAT WAS BEHIND THOSE CARING EYES...
BUT NOW I KNOW THAT HIS SLEEPING VIGIL AT MY BEDSIDE WAS HIS WAY OF SAYING...
"I LOVE YOU... YOU'RE THE CHILD I COULD NEVER LIVE WITHOUT..."
YEARS LATER, I BLOSSOMED INTO A "LITTLE LAMIA."
I WANTED SO MUCH TO BE EXACTLY LIKE MY MOTHER.
I'D MIRROR EVERYTHING SHE DID... TO A T...

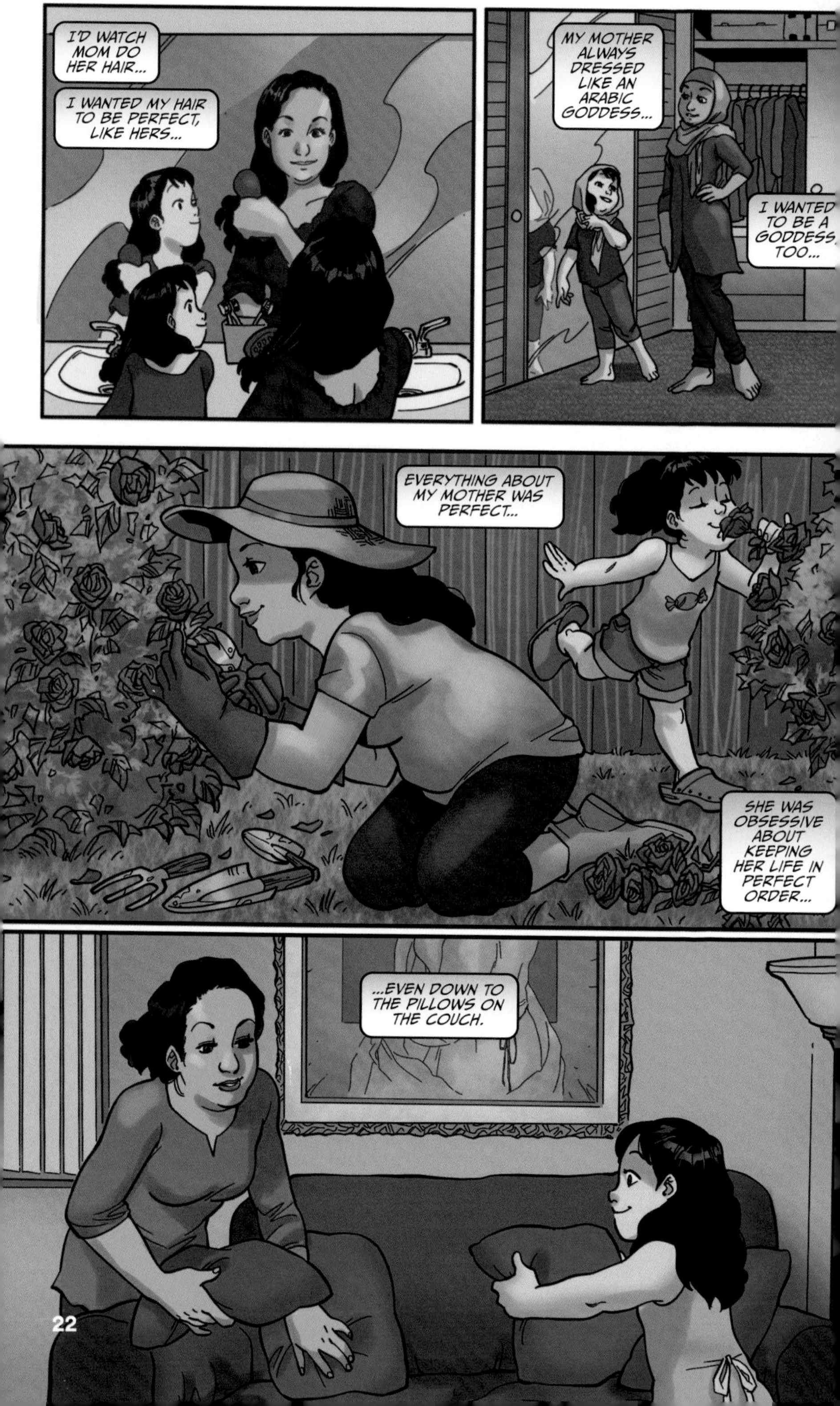
I'D WATCH MOM DO HER HAIR...
I WANTED MY HAIR TO BE PERFECT, LIKE HERS...
MY MOTHER ALWAYS DRESSED LIKE AN ARABIC GODDESS...
I WANTED TO BE A GODDESS, TOO...
EVERYTHING ABOUT MY MOTHER WAS PERFECT...
SHE WAS OBSESSIVE ABOUT KEEPING HER LIFE IN PERFECT ORDER...
...EVEN DOWN TO THE PILLOWS ON THE COUCH.

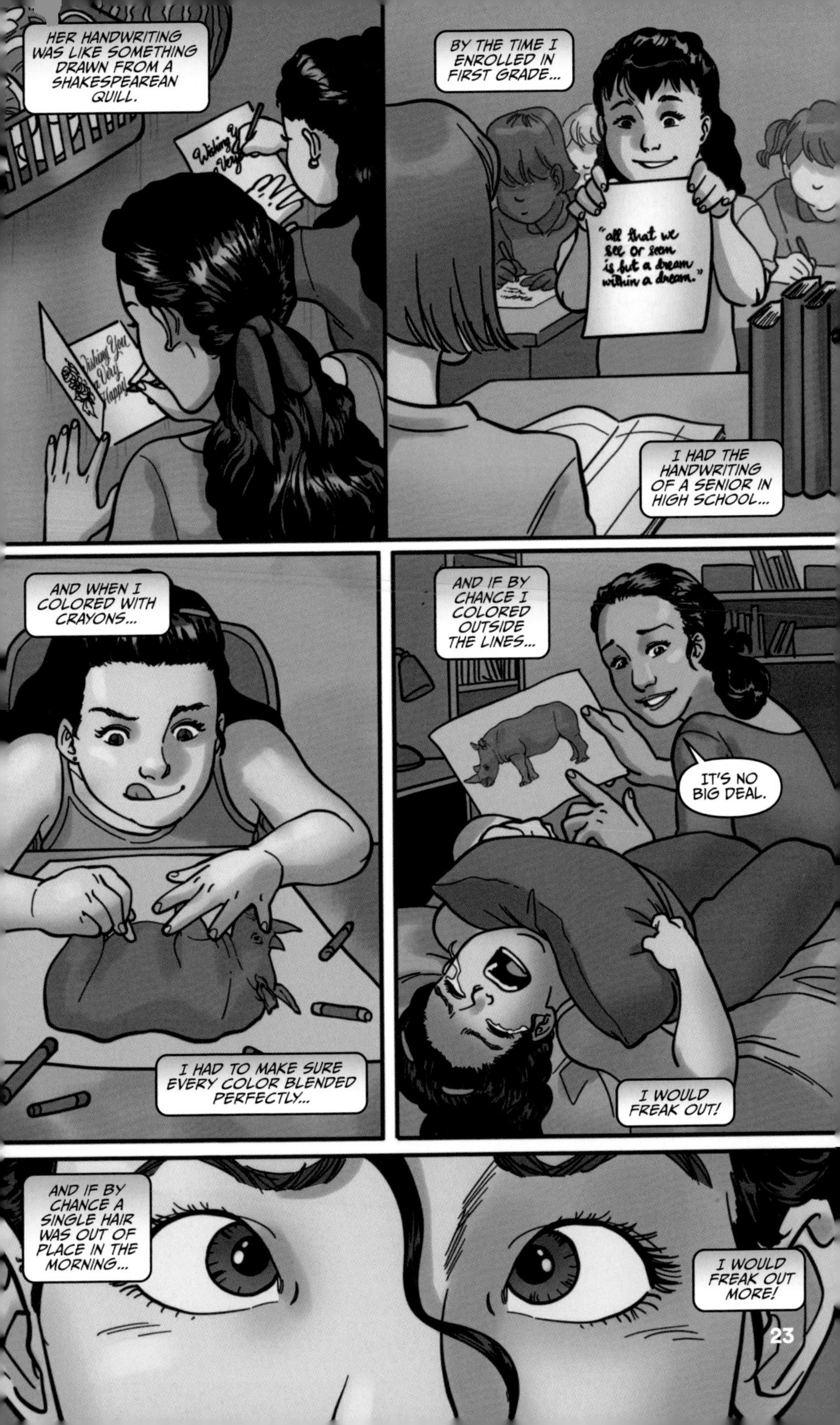
HER HANDWRITING WAS LIKE SOMETHING DRAWN FROM A SHAKESPEAREAN QUILL.
Wishing You a Very Happy
BY THE TIME I ENROLLED IN FIRST GRADE...
"all that we see or seem is but a dream within a dream."
I HAD THE HANDWRITING OF A SENIOR IN HIGH SCHOOL...
AND WHEN I COLORED WITH CRAYONS...
I HAD TO MAKE SURE EVERY COLOR BLENDED PERFECTLY...
AND IF BY CHANCE I COLORED OUTSIDE THE LINES...
IT'S NO BIG DEAL.
I WOULD FREAK OUT!
AND IF BY CHANCE A SINGLE HAIR WAS OUT OF PLACE IN THE MORNING...
I WOULD FREAK OUT MORE!

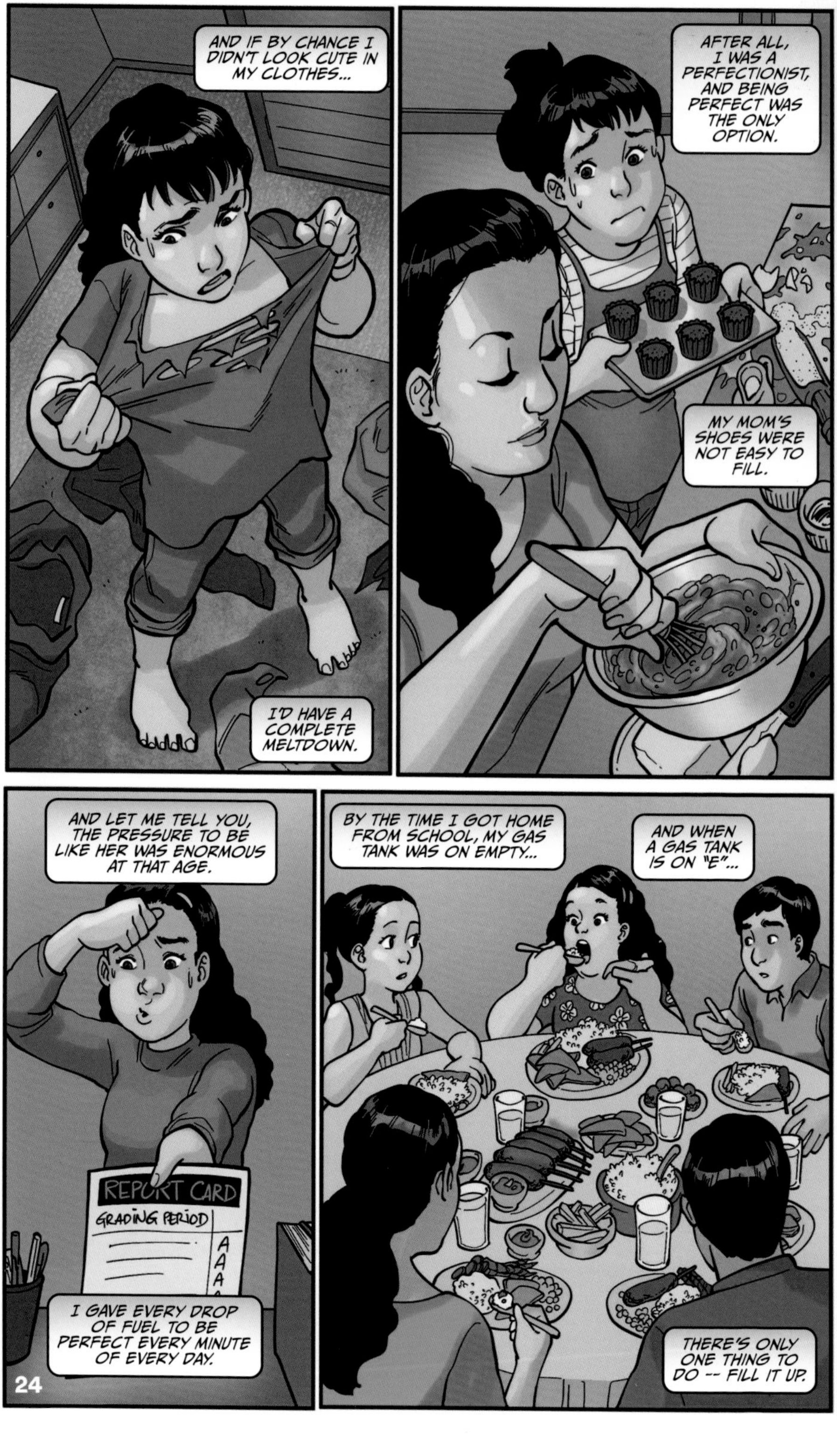
AND IF BY CHANCE I DIDN'T LOOK CUTE IN MY CLOTHES...
I'D HAVE A COMPLETE MELTDOWN.
AFTER ALL, I WAS A PERFECTIONIST, AND BEING PERFECT WAS THE ONLY OPTION.
MY MOM'S SHOES WERE NOT EASY TO FILL.
AND LET ME TELL YOU, THE PRESSURE TO BE LIKE HER WAS ENORMOUS AT THAT AGE.
REPORT CARD
GRADING PERIOD
A
A
A
I GAVE EVERY DROP OF FUEL TO BE PERFECT EVERY MINUTE OF EVERY DAY.
BY THE TIME I GOT HOME FROM SCHOOL, MY GAS TANK WAS ON EMPTY...
AND WHEN A GAS TANK IS ON "E"...
THERE'S ONLY ONE THING TO DO -- FILL IT UP.

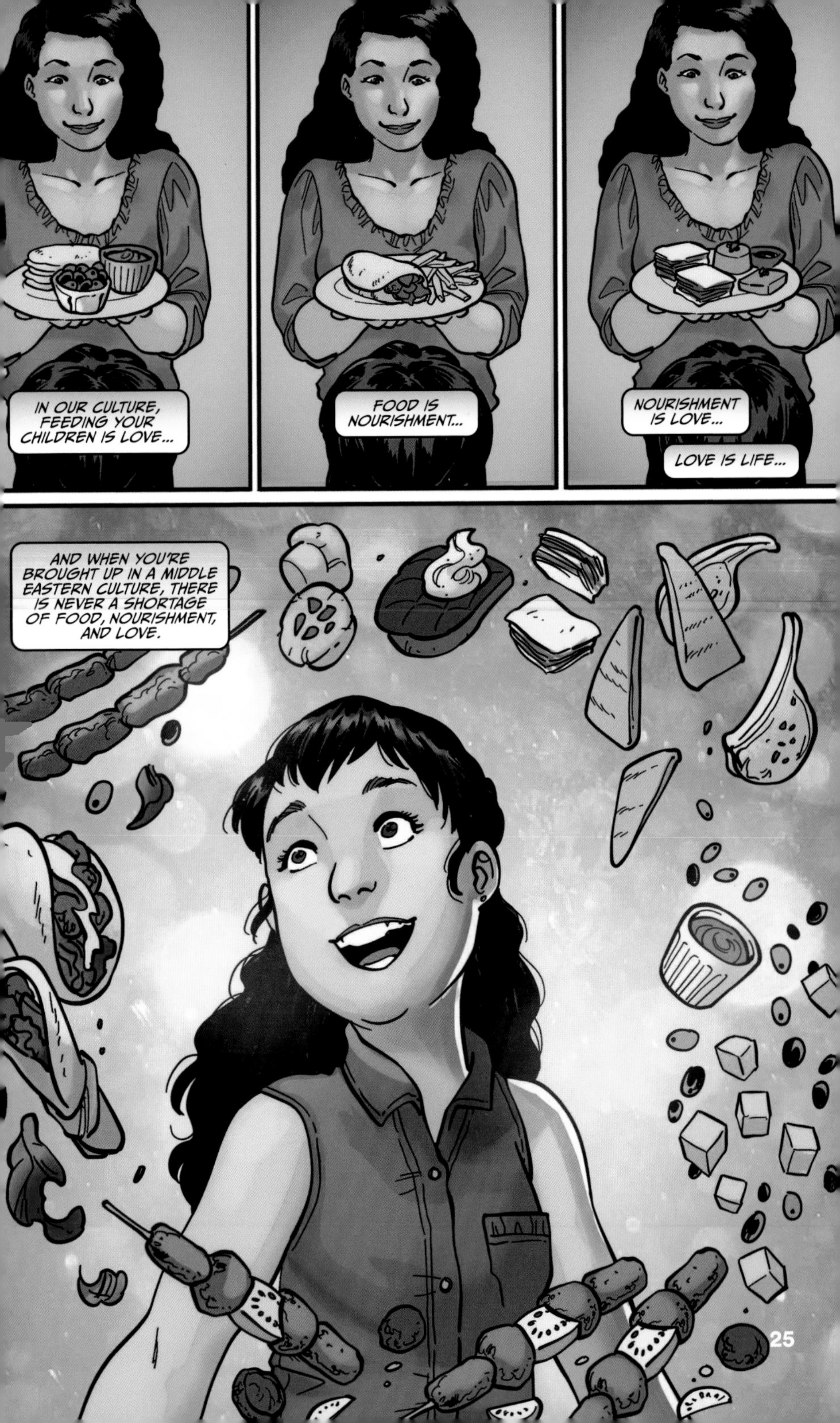

IN OUR CULTURE, FEEDING YOUR CHILDREN IS LOVE...
FOOD IS NOURISHMENT...
NOURISHMENT IS LOVE...
LOVE IS LIFE...
AND WHEN YOU'RE BROUGHT UP IN A MIDDLE EASTERN CULTURE, THERE IS NEVER A SHORTAGE OF FOOD, NOURISHMENT, AND LOVE.

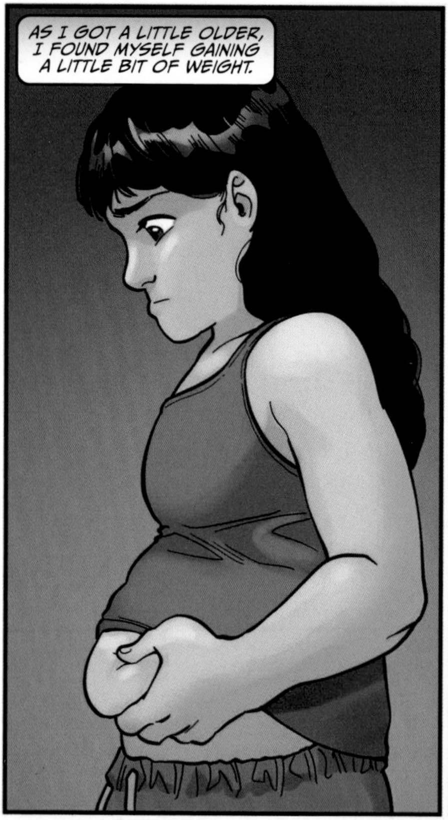
AS I GOT A LITTLE OLDER, I FOUND MYSELF GAINING A LITTLE BIT OF WEIGHT.

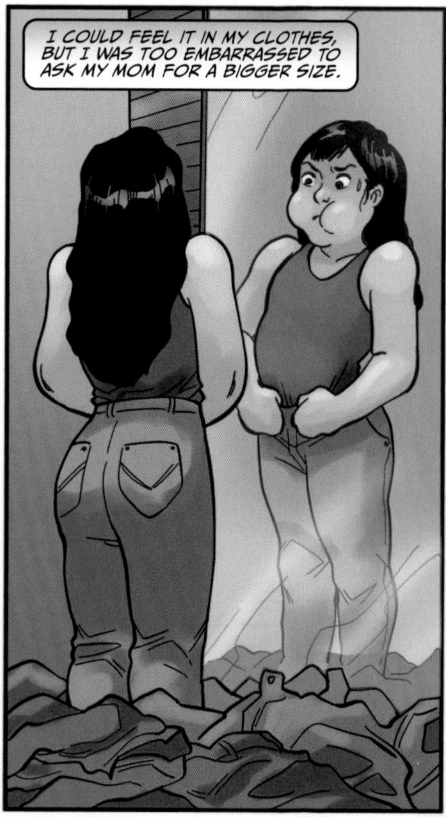
I COULD FEEL IT IN MY CLOTHES, BUT I WAS TOO EMBARRASSED TO ASK MY MOM FOR A BIGGER SIZE.

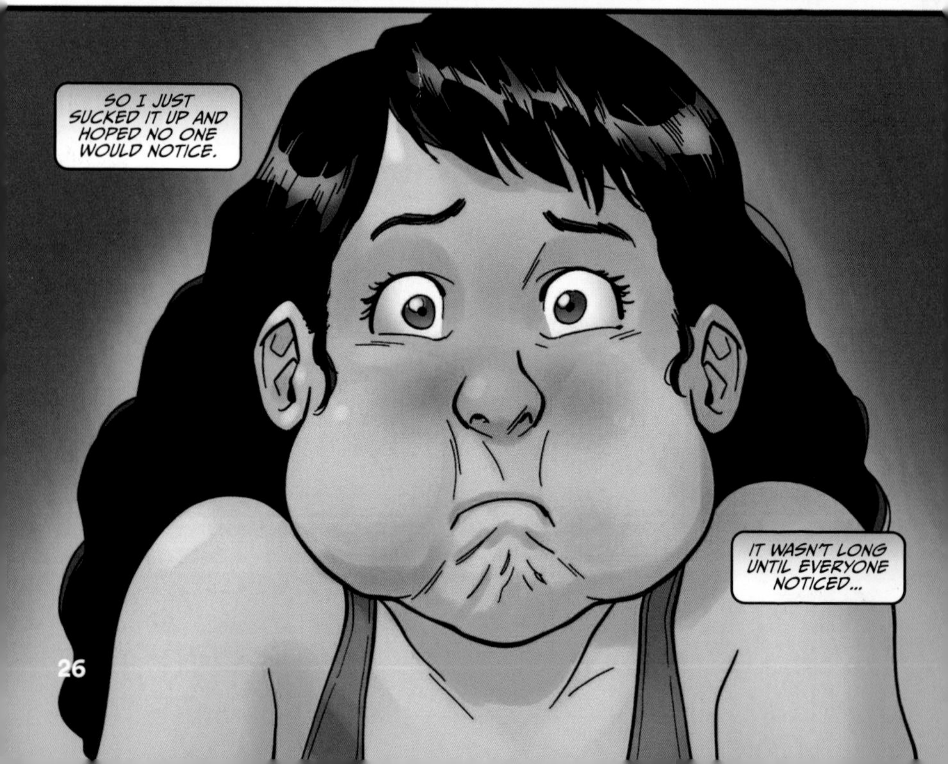
SO I JUST SUCKED IT UP AND HOPED NO ONE WOULD NOTICE.
IT WASN'T LONG UNTIL EVERYONE NOTICED...

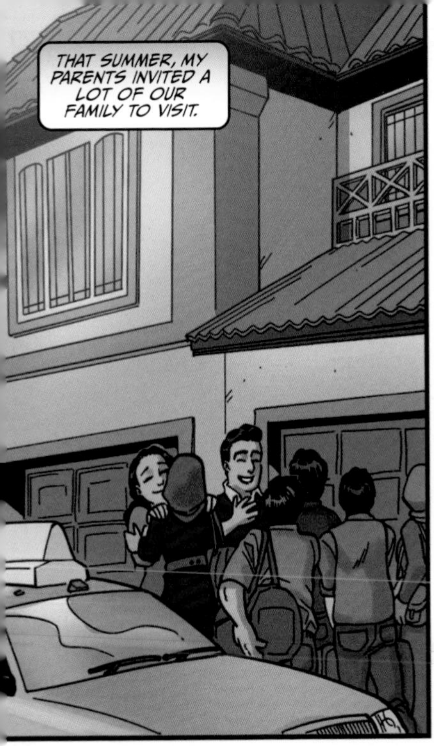
THAT SUMMER, MY PARENTS INVITED A LOT OF OUR FAMILY TO VISIT.

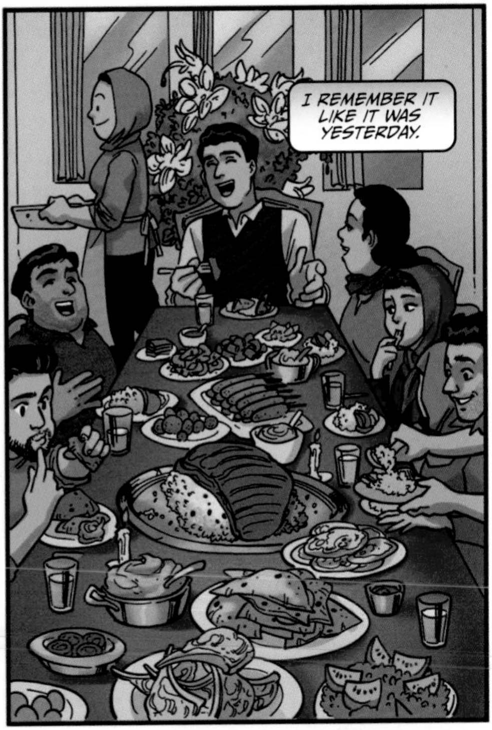
I REMEMBER IT LIKE IT WAS YESTERDAY.

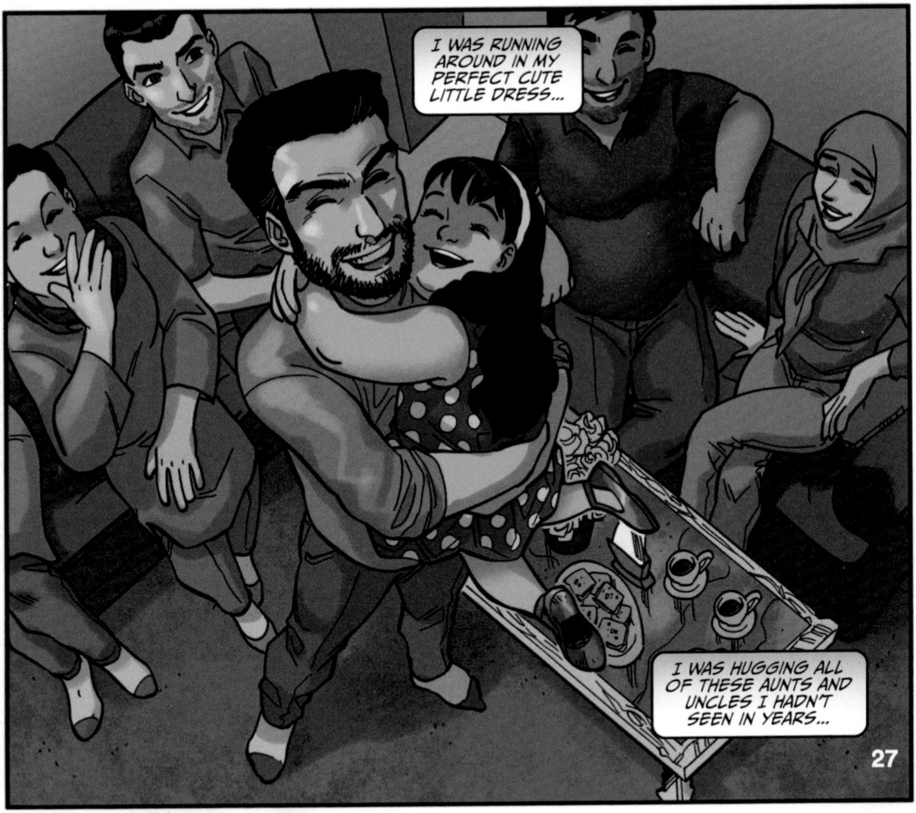
I WAS RUNNING AROUND IN MY PERFECT CUTE LITTLE DRESS...
I WAS HUGGING ALL OF THESE AUNTS AND UNCLES I HADN'T SEEN IN YEARS...

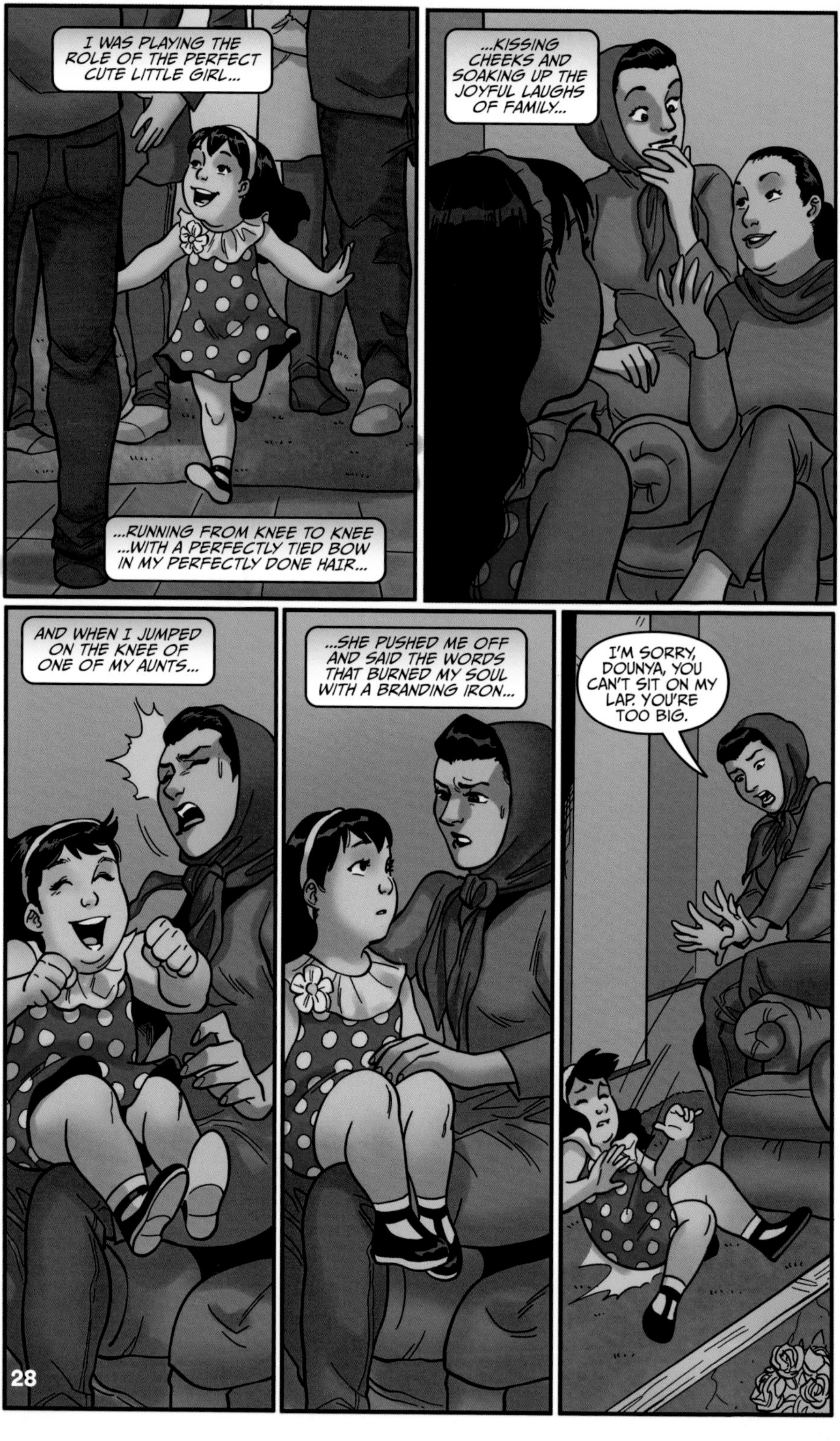
I WAS PLAYING THE ROLE OF THE PERFECT CUTE LITTLE GIRL...
...RUNNING FROM KNEE TO KNEE ...WITH A PERFECTLY TIED BOW IN MY PERFECTLY DONE HAIR...
...KISSING CHEEKS AND SOAKING UP THE JOYFUL LAUGHS OF FAMILY...
AND WHEN I JUMPED ON THE KNEE OF ONE OF MY AUNTS...
...SHE PUSHED ME OFF AND SAID THE WORDS THAT BURNED MY SOUL WITH A BRANDING IRON...
I'M SORRY, DOUNYA, YOU CAN'T SIT ON MY LAP. YOU'RE TOO BIG.

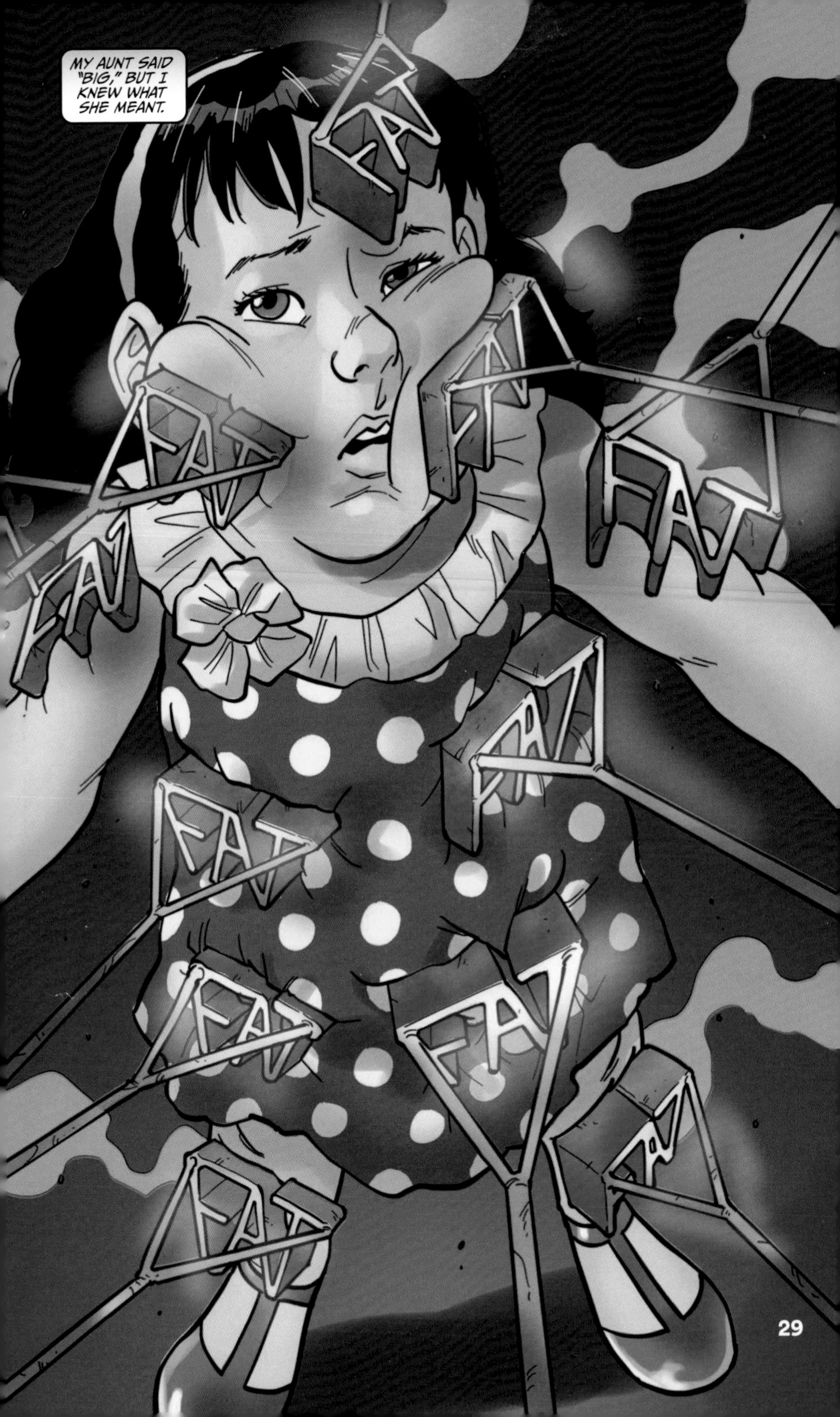
MY AUNT SAID "BIG," BUT I KNEW WHAT SHE MEANT.

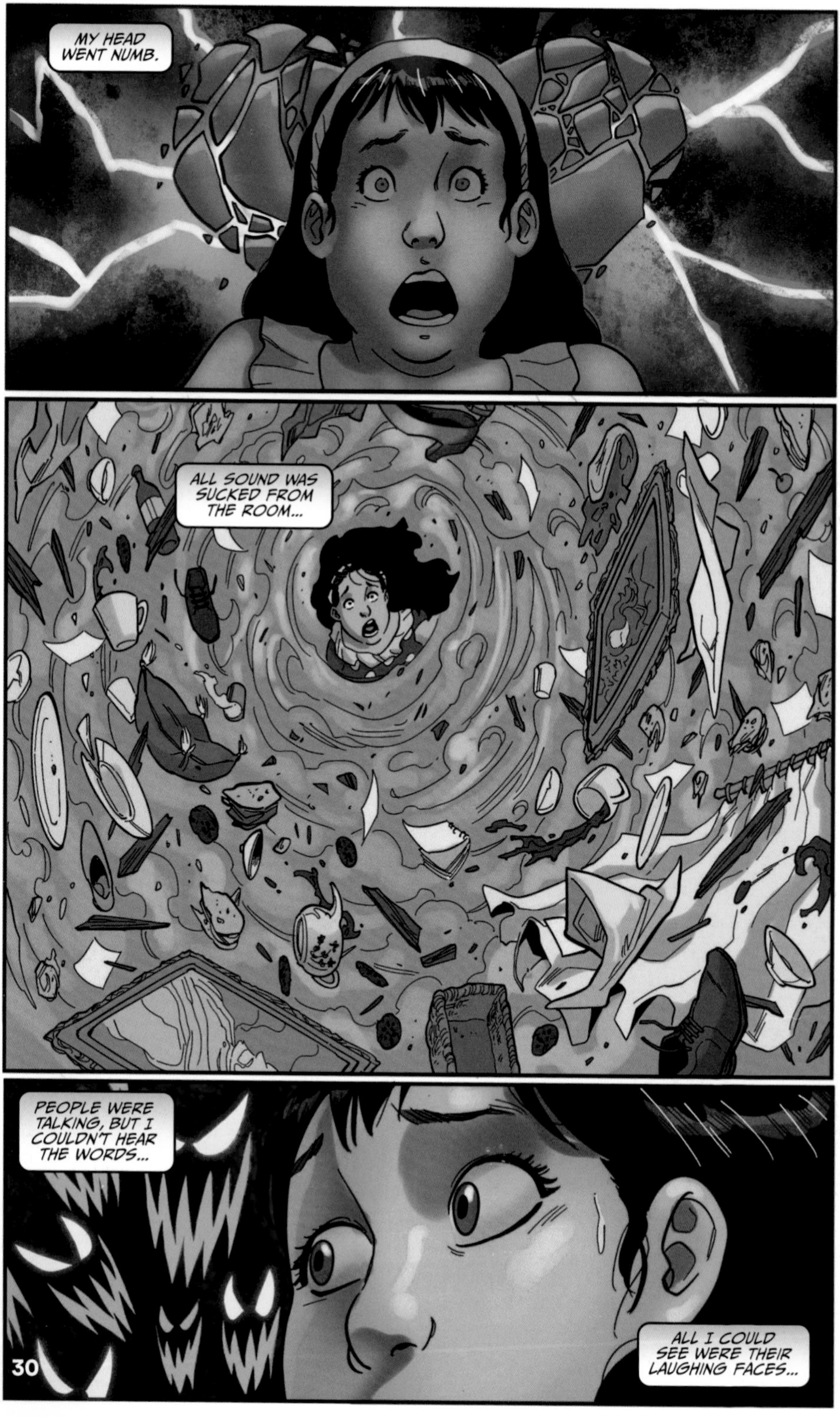
MY HEAD WENT NUMB.
ALL SOUND WAS SUCKED FROM THE ROOM...
PEOPLE WERE TALKING, BUT I COULDN'T HEAR THE WORDS...
ALL I COULD SEE WERE THEIR LAUGHING FACES...

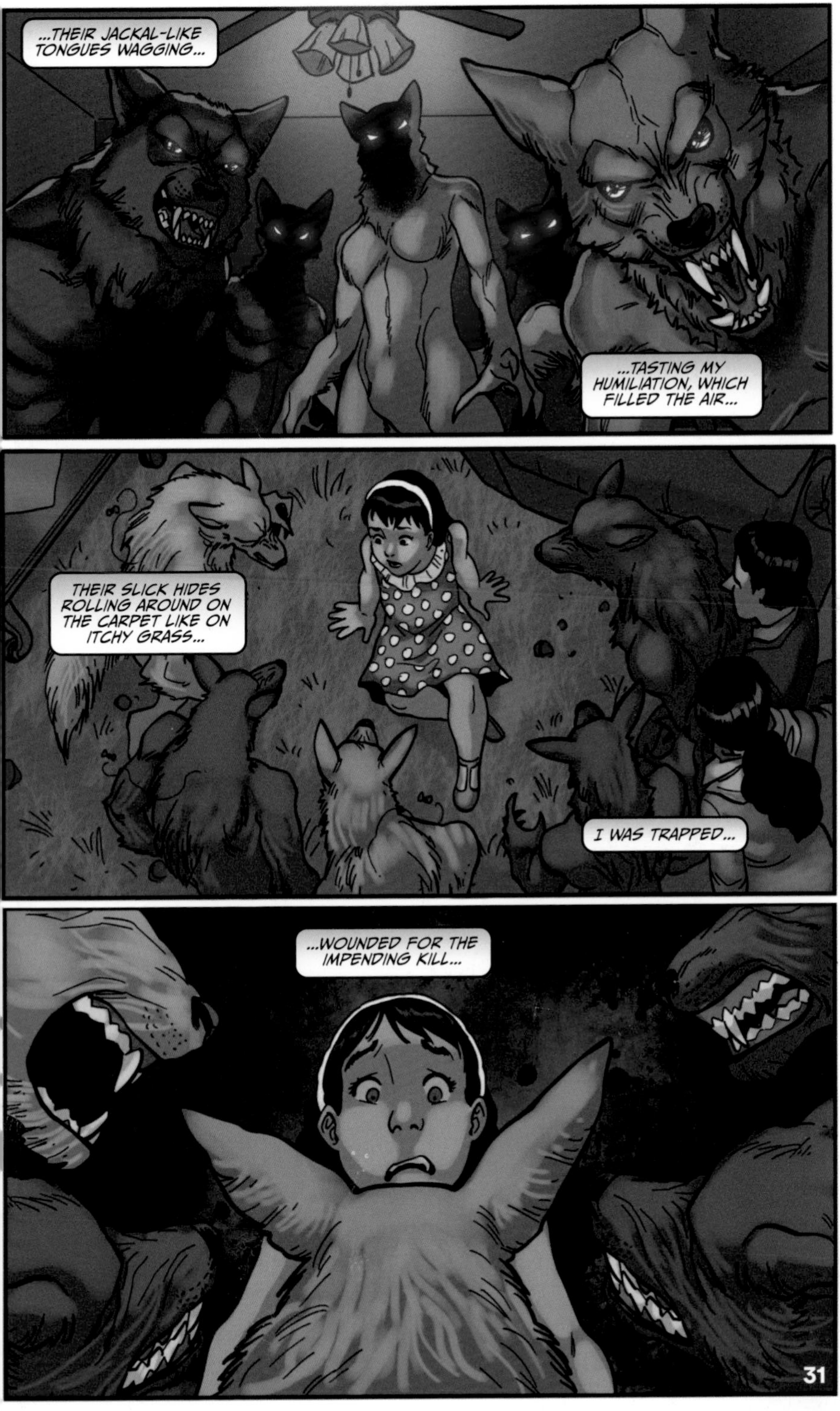

...THEIR JACKAL-LIKE TONGUES WAGGING...
...TASTING MY HUMILIATION, WHICH FILLED THE AIR...
THEIR SLICK HIDES ROLLING AROUND ON THE CARPET LIKE ON ITCHY GRASS...
I WAS TRAPPED...
...WOUNDED FOR THE IMPENDING KILL...

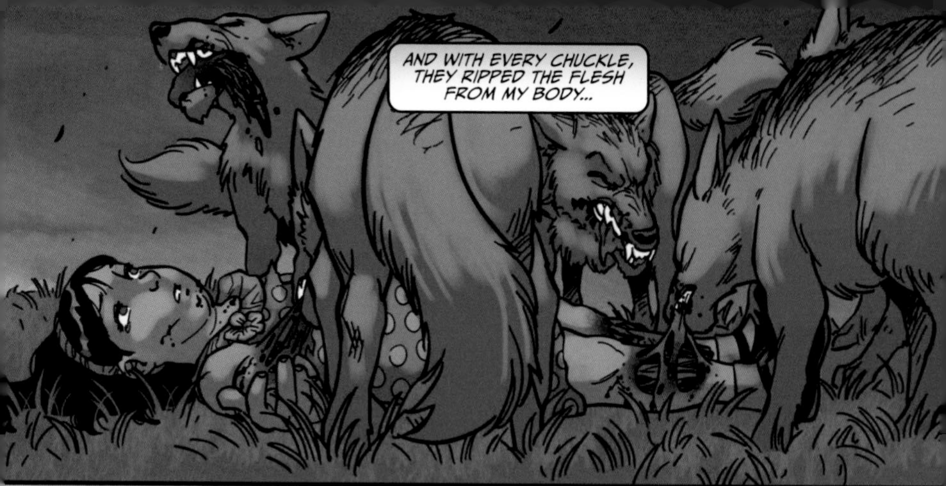
AND WITH EVERY CHUCKLE, THEY RIPPED THE FLESH FROM MY BODY...

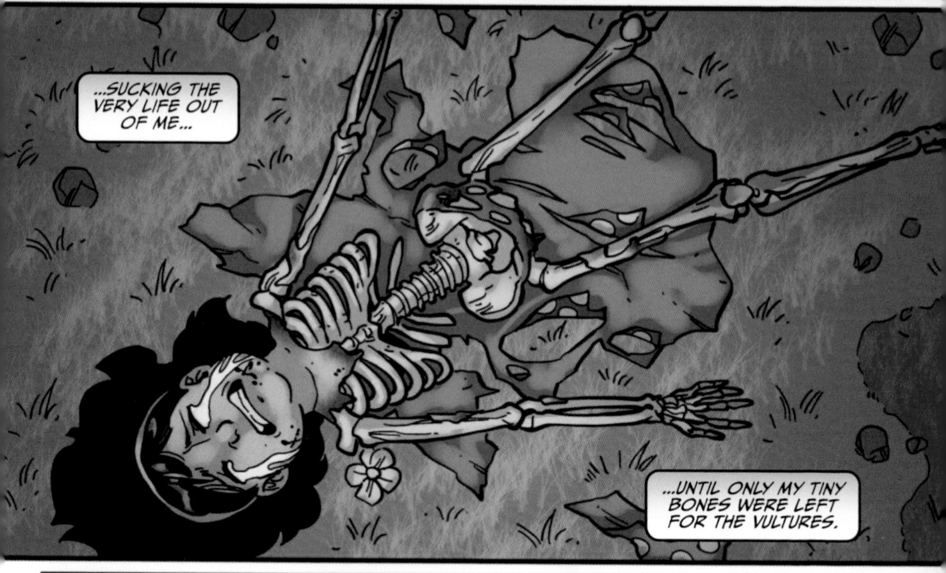
...SUCKING THE VERY LIFE OUT OF ME...
...UNTIL ONLY MY TINY BONES WERE LEFT FOR THE VULTURES.

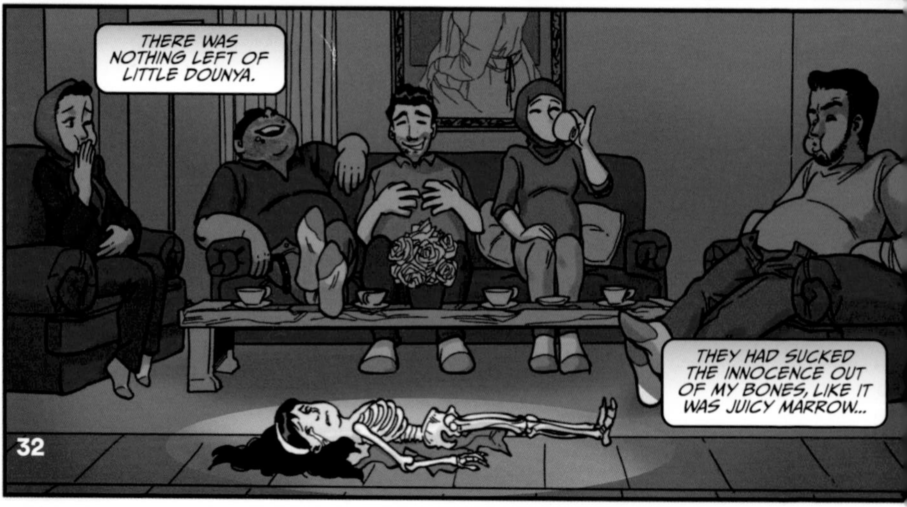
THERE WAS NOTHING LEFT OF LITTLE DOUNYA.
THEY HAD SUCKED THE INNOCENCE OUT OF MY BONES, LIKE IT WAS JUICY MARROW...

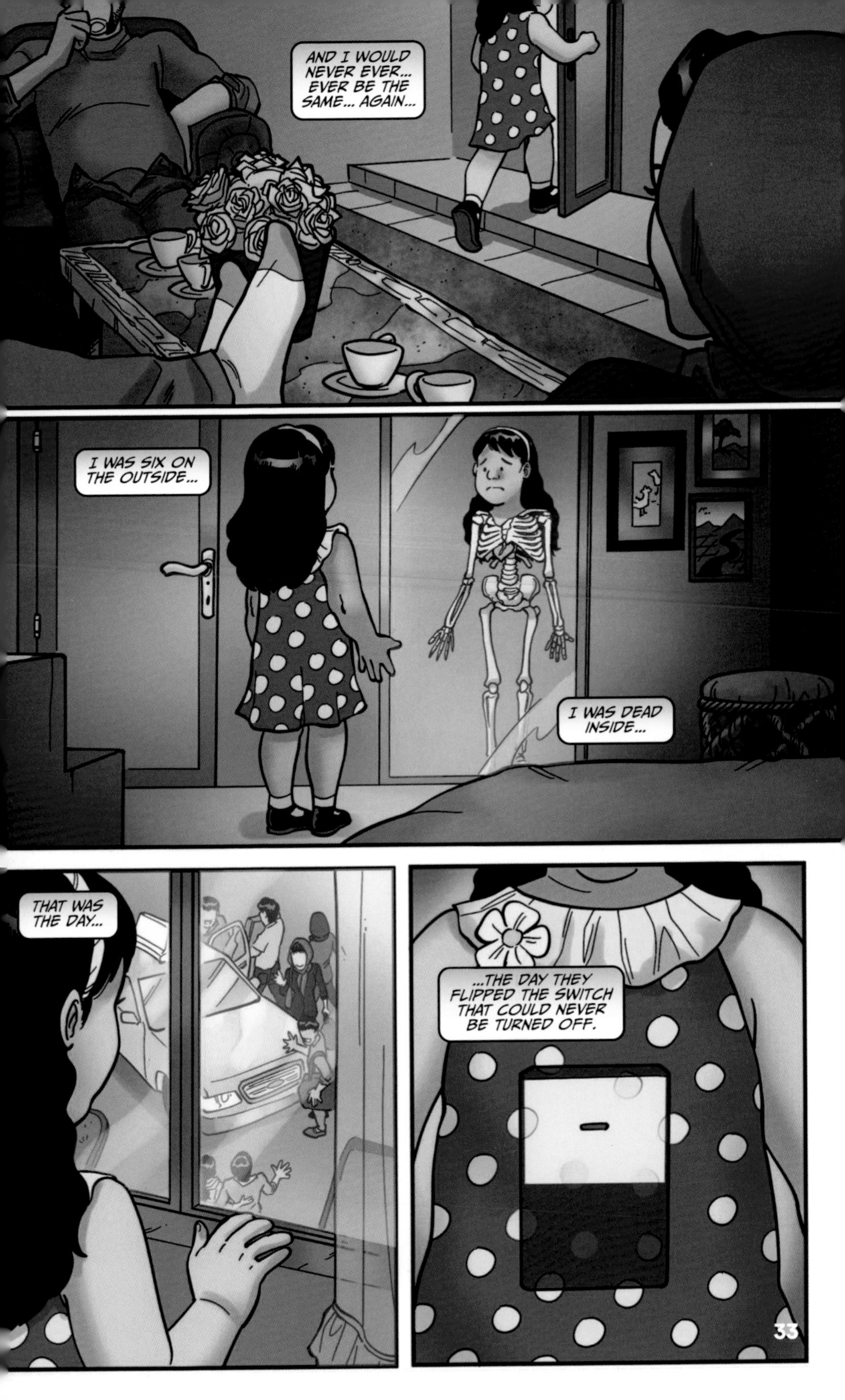
AND I WOULD NEVER EVER... EVER BE THE SAME... AGAIN...
I WAS SIX ON THE OUTSIDE...
I WAS DEAD INSIDE...
THAT WAS THE DAY...
...THE DAY THEY FLIPPED THE SWITCH THAT COULD NEVER BE TURNED OFF.

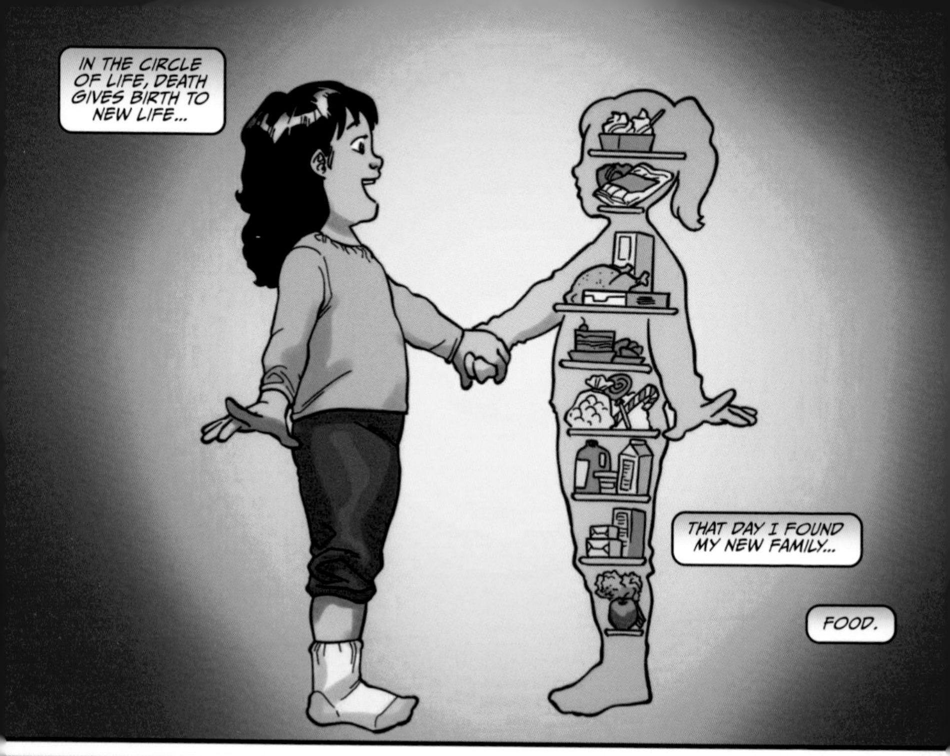
IN THE CIRCLE OF LIFE, DEATH GIVES BIRTH TO NEW LIFE...
THAT DAY I FOUND MY NEW FAMILY...
FOOD.

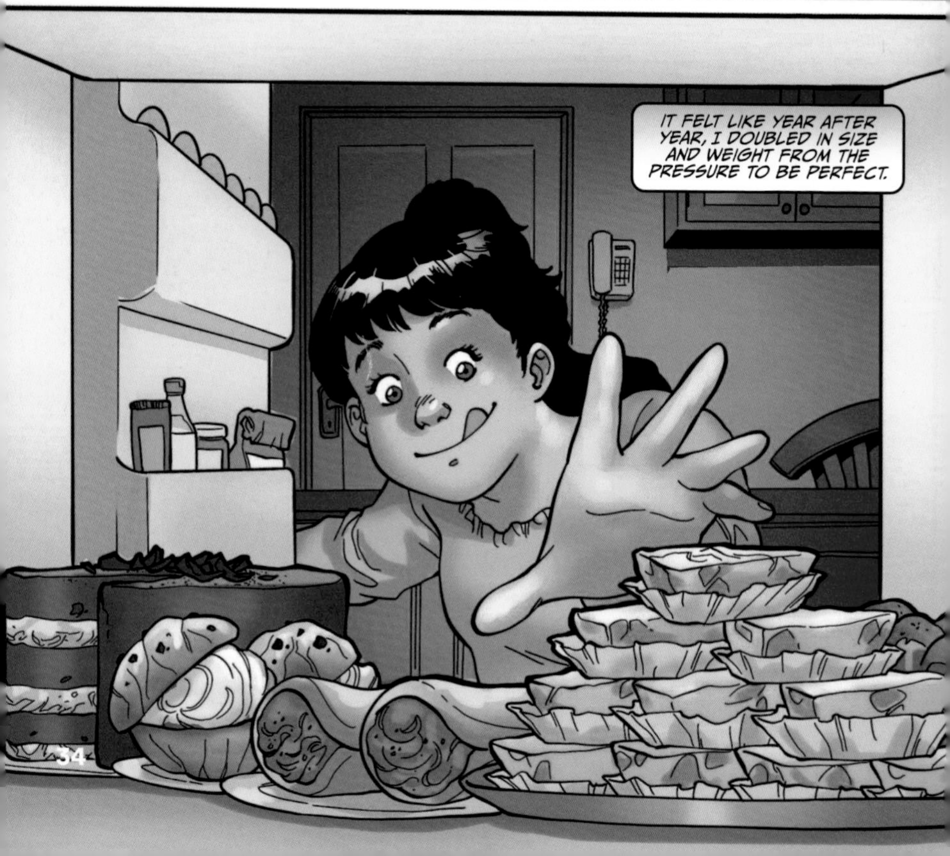
IT FELT LIKE YEAR AFTER YEAR, I DOUBLED IN SIZE AND WEIGHT FROM THE PRESSURE TO BE PERFECT.

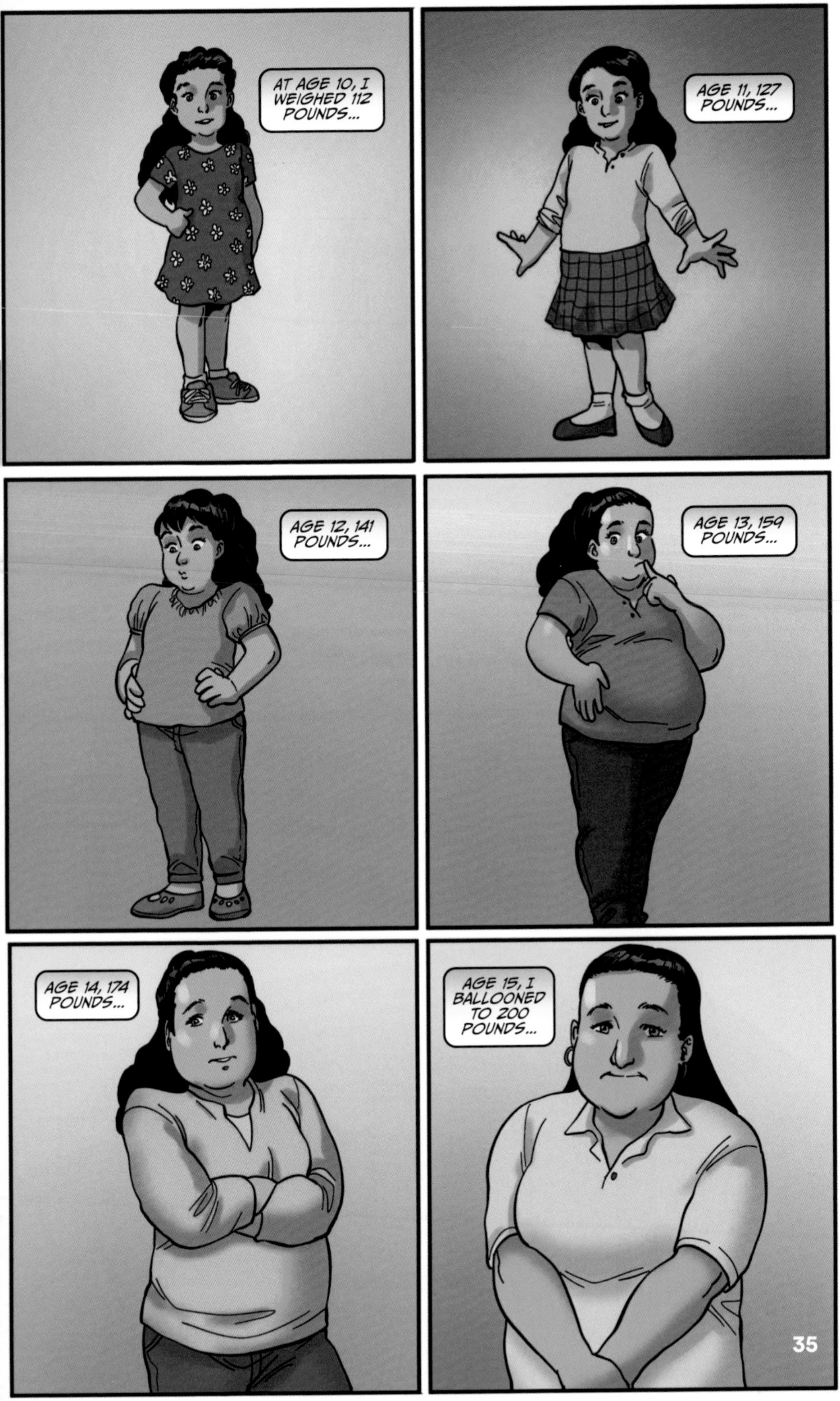
AT AGE 10, I WEIGHED 112 POUNDS...
AGE 11, 127 POUNDS...
AGE 12, 141 POUNDS...
AGE 13, 159 POUNDS...
AGE 14, 174 POUNDS...
AGE 15, I BALLOONED TO 200 POUNDS...

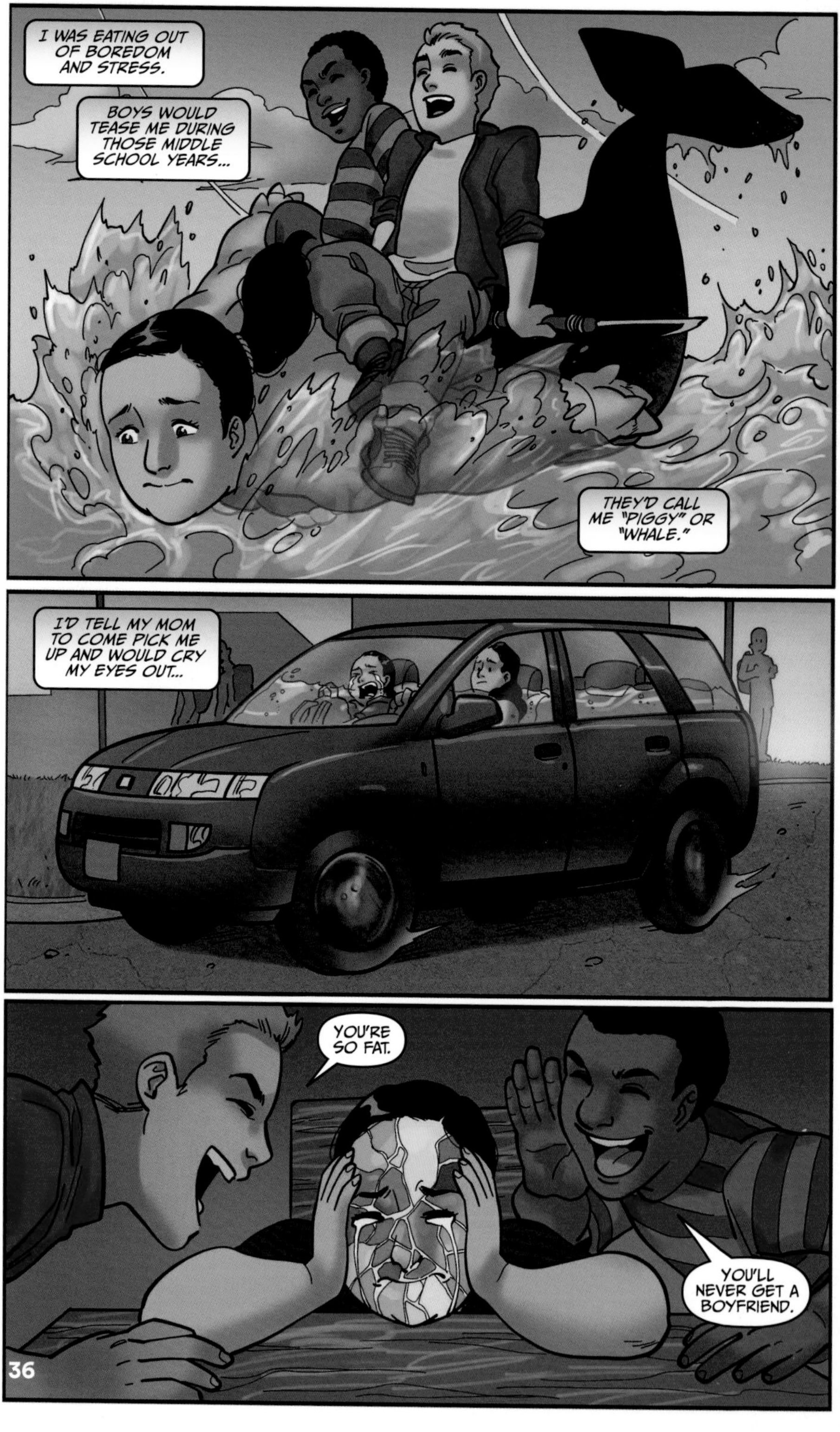
I WAS EATING OUT OF BOREDOM AND STRESS.
BOYS WOULD TEASE ME DURING THOSE MIDDLE SCHOOL YEARS...
THEY'D CALL ME "PIGGY" OR "WHALE."
I'D TELL MY MOM TO COME PICK ME UP AND WOULD CRY MY EYES OUT...
YOU'RE SO FAT.
YOU'LL NEVER GET A BOYFRIEND.

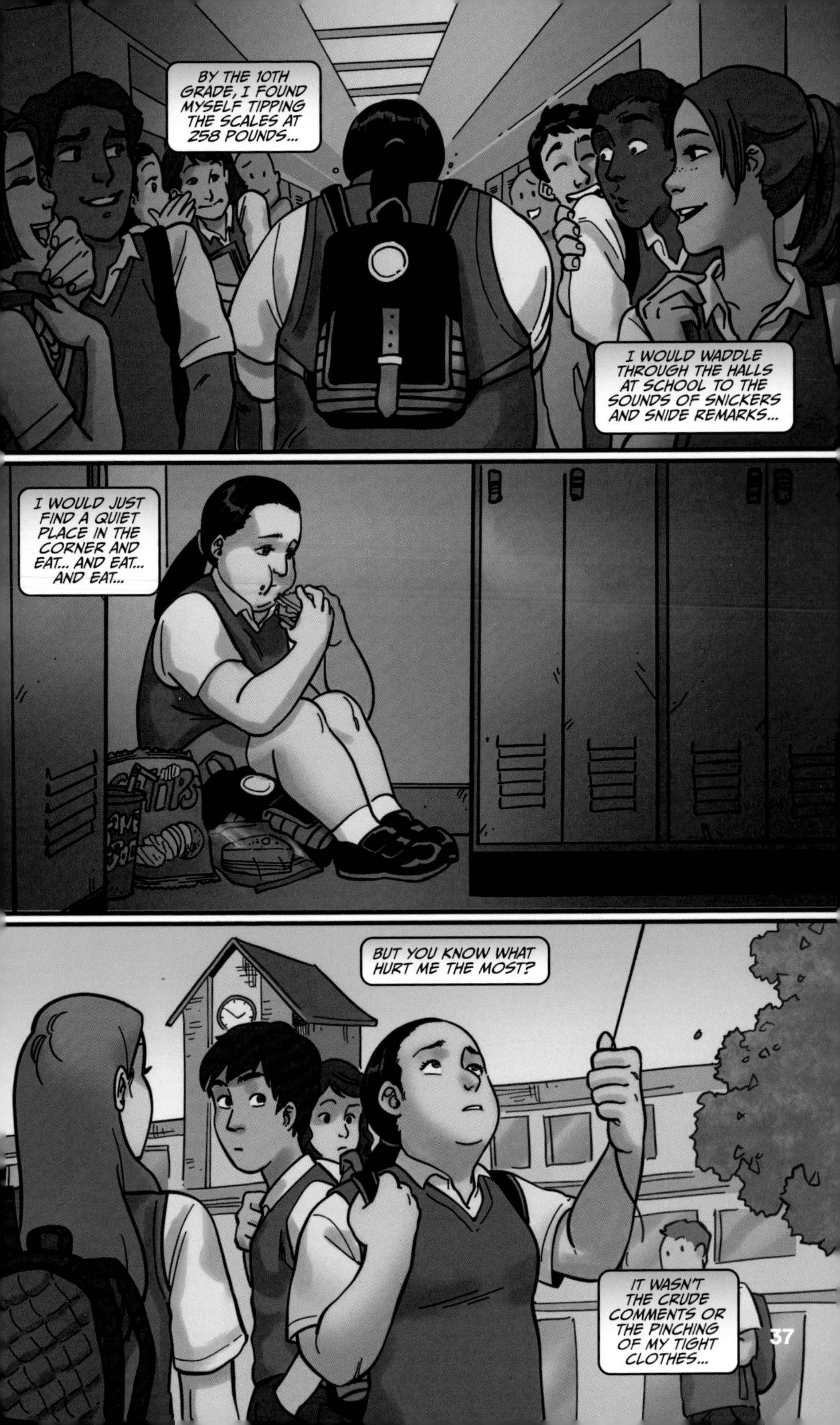

BY THE 10TH GRADE, I FOUND MYSELF TIPPING THE SCALES AT 258 POUNDS...
I WOULD WADDLE THROUGH THE HALLS AT SCHOOL TO THE SOUNDS OF SNICKERS AND SNIDE REMARKS...
I WOULD JUST FIND A QUIET PLACE IN THE CORNER AND EAT... AND EAT... AND EAT...
BUT YOU KNOW WHAT HURT ME THE MOST?
IT WASN'T THE CRUDE COMMENTS OR THE PINCHING OF MY TIGHT CLOTHES...

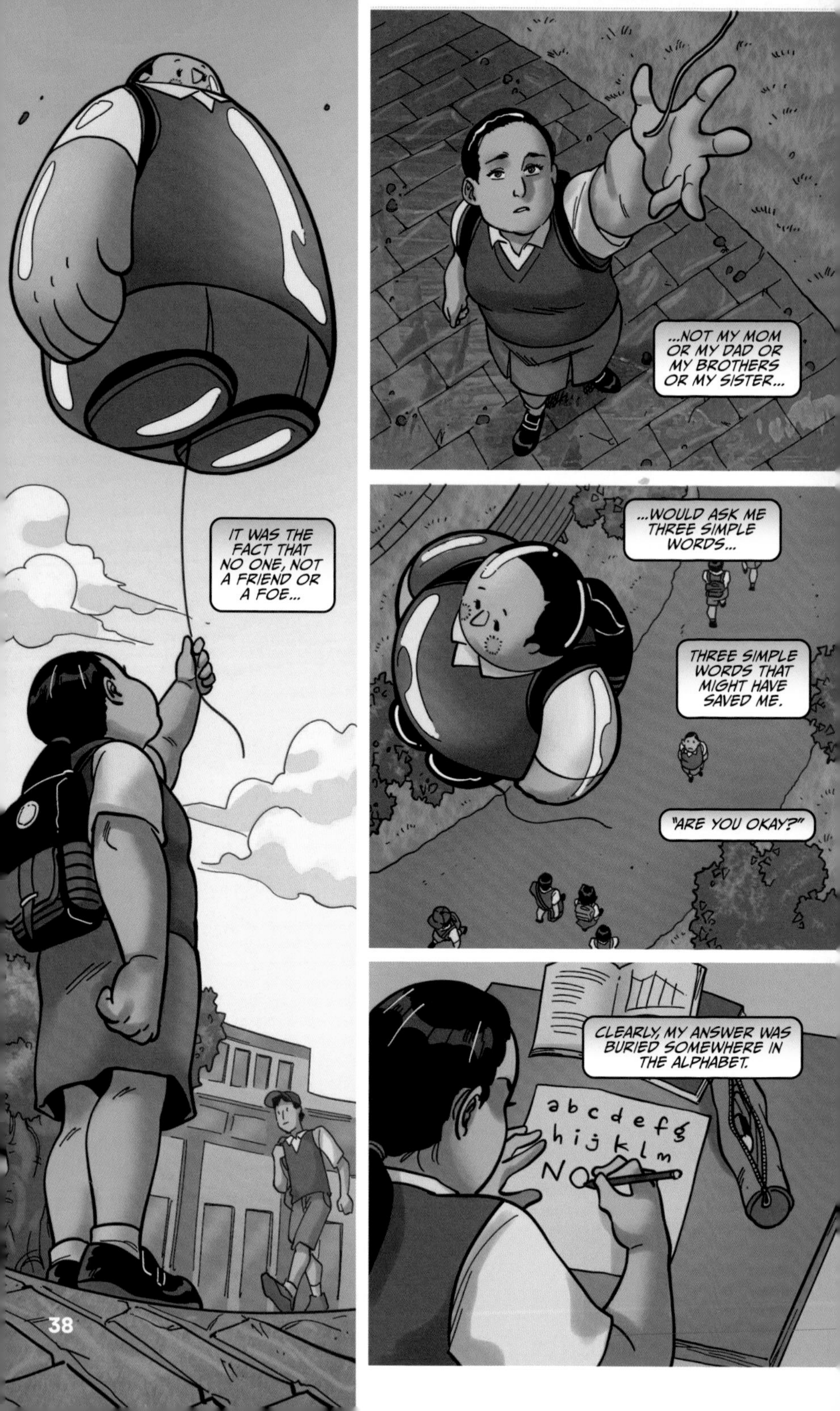
IT WAS THE FACT THAT NO ONE, NOT A FRIEND OR A FOE...
...NOT MY MOM OR MY DAD OR MY BROTHERS OR MY SISTER...
...WOULD ASK ME THREE SIMPLE WORDS...
THREE SIMPLE WORDS THAT MIGHT HAVE SAVED ME.
"ARE YOU OKAY?"
CLEARLY, MY ANSWER WAS BURIED SOMEWHERE IN THE ALPHABET.
abcdefg
hijklm
NO

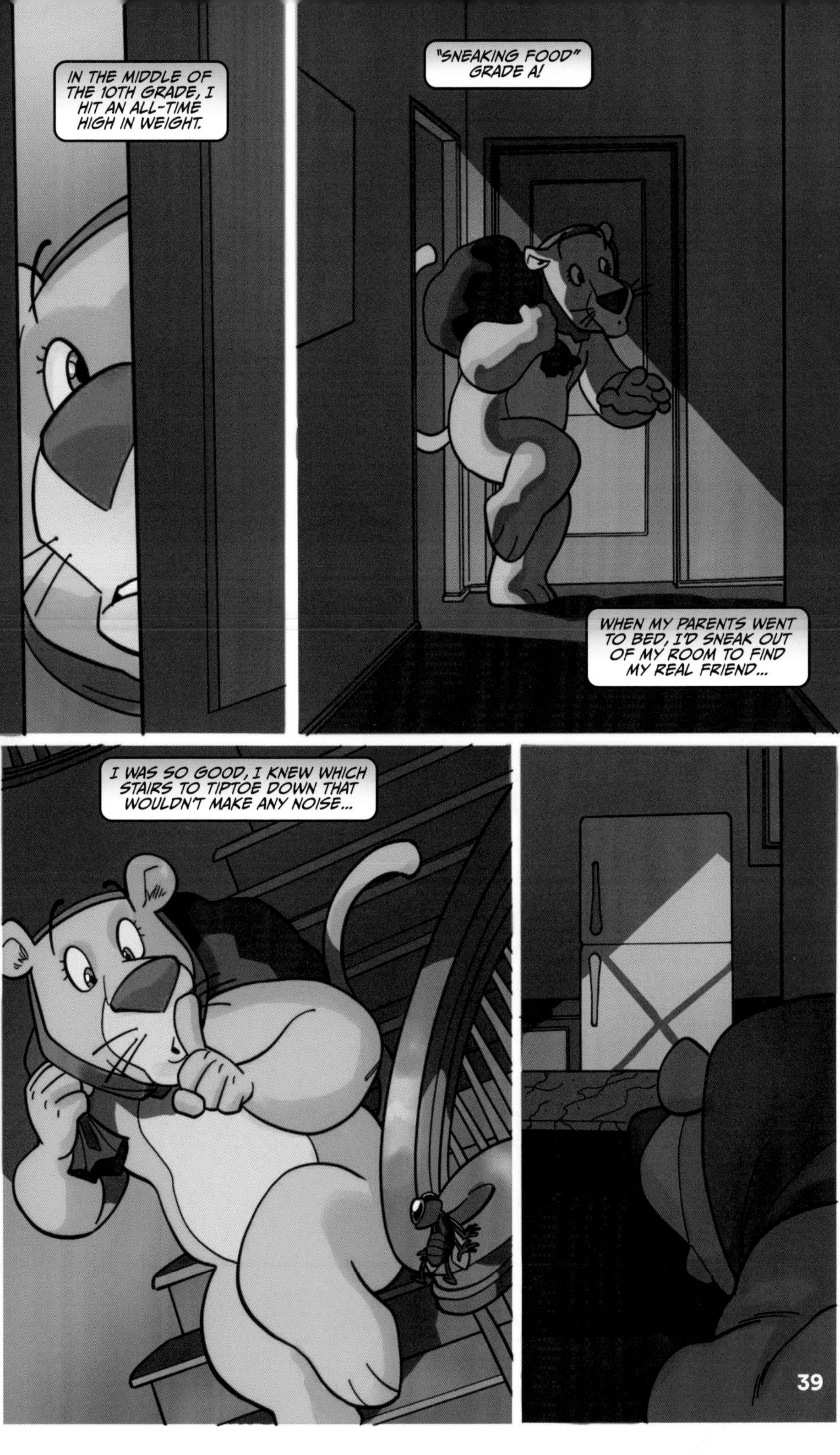
IN THE MIDDLE OF THE 10TH GRADE, I HIT AN ALL-TIME HIGH IN WEIGHT.
"SNEAKING FOOD" GRADE A!
WHEN MY PARENTS WENT TO BED, I'D SNEAK OUT OF MY ROOM TO FIND MY REAL FRIEND...
I WAS SO GOOD, I KNEW WHICH STAIRS TO TIPTOE DOWN THAT WOULDN'T MAKE ANY NOISE...

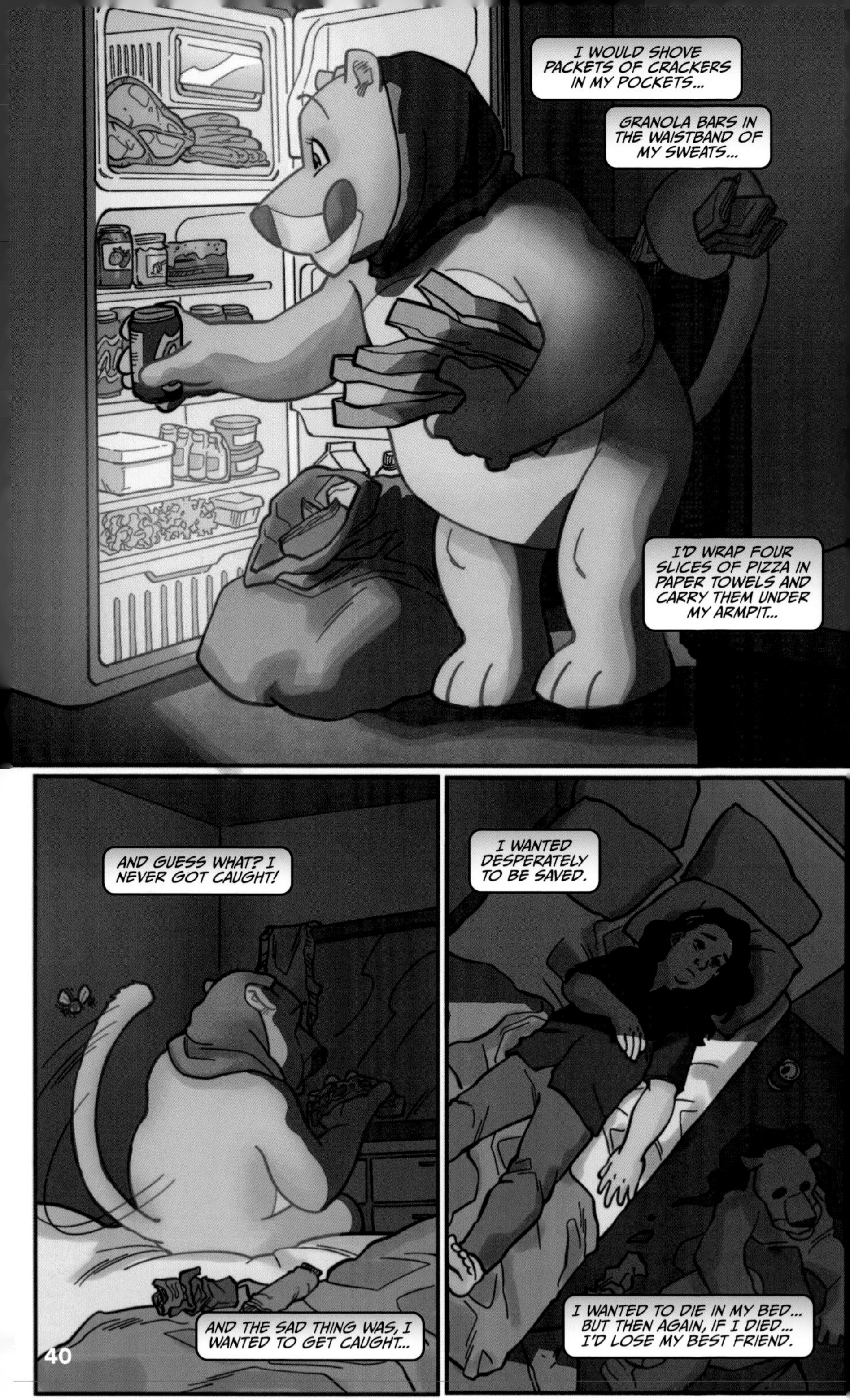
I WOULD SHOVE PACKETS OF CRACKERS IN MY POCKETS...
GRANOLA BARS IN THE WAISTBAND OF MY SWEATS...
I'D WRAP FOUR SLICES OF PIZZA IN PAPER TOWELS AND CARRY THEM UNDER MY ARMPIT...
AND GUESS WHAT? I NEVER GOT CAUGHT!
AND THE SAD THING WAS, I WANTED TO GET CAUGHT...
I WANTED DESPERATELY TO BE SAVED.
I WANTED TO DIE IN MY BED... BUT THEN AGAIN, IF I DIED... I'D LOSE MY BEST FRIEND.

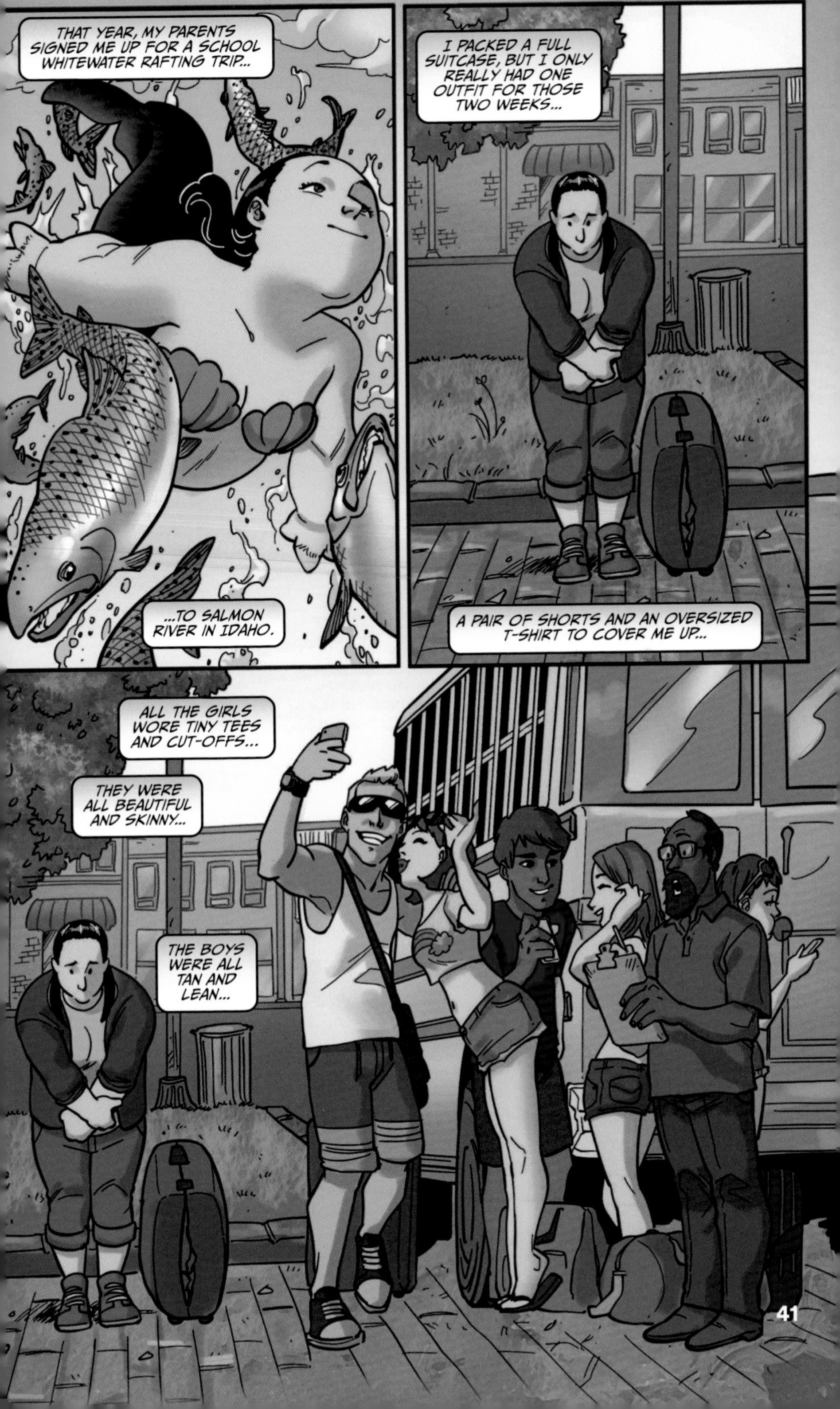
THAT YEAR, MY PARENTS SIGNED ME UP FOR A SCHOOL WHITEWATER RAFTING TRIP...
...TO SALMON RIVER IN IDAHO.
I PACKED A FULL SUITCASE, BUT I ONLY REALLY HAD ONE OUTFIT FOR THOSE TWO WEEKS...
A PAIR OF SHORTS AND AN OVERSIZED T-SHIRT TO COVER ME UP...
ALL THE GIRLS WORE TINY TEES AND CUT-OFFS...
THEY WERE ALL BEAUTIFUL AND SKINNY...
THE BOYS WERE ALL TAN AND LEAN...

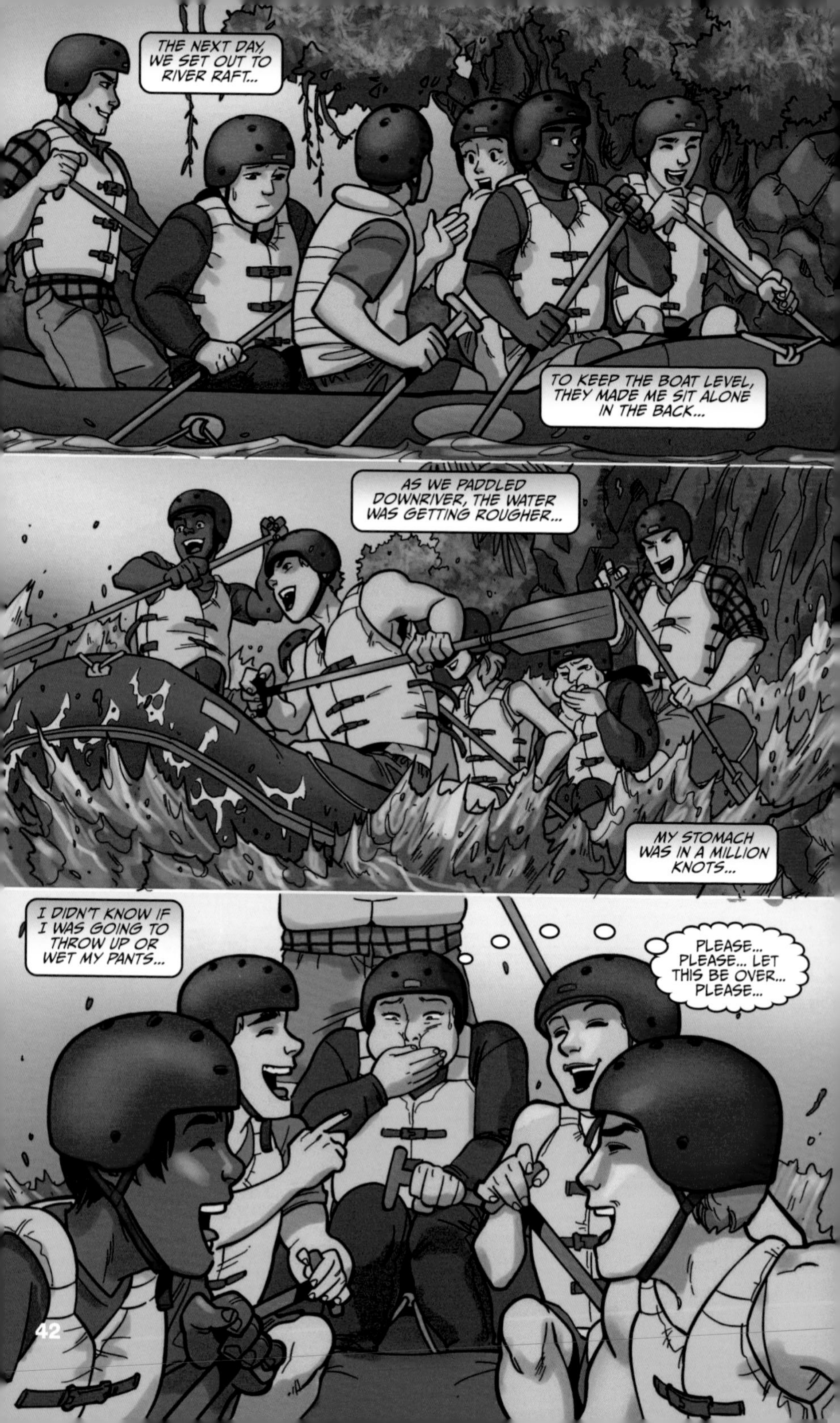
THE NEXT DAY, WE SET OUT TO RIVER RAFT...
TO KEEP THE BOAT LEVEL, THEY MADE ME SIT ALONE IN THE BACK...
AS WE PADDLED DOWNRIVER, THE WATER WAS GETTING ROUGHER...
MY STOMACH WAS IN A MILLION KNOTS...
I DIDN'T KNOW IF I WAS GOING TO THROW UP OR WET MY PANTS...
PLEASE... PLEASE... LET THIS BE OVER... PLEASE...

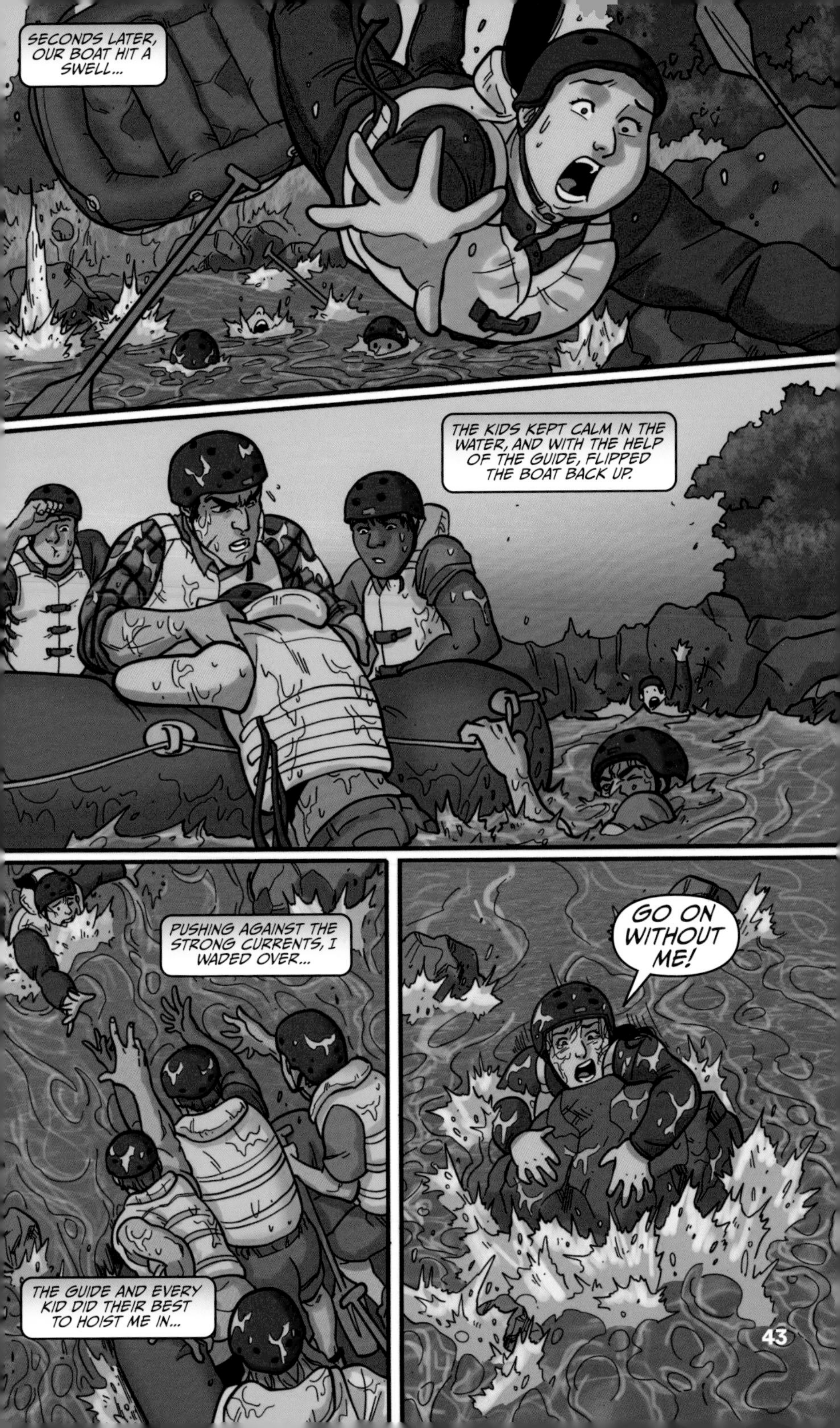
SECONDS LATER, OUR BOAT HIT A SWELL...
THE KIDS KEPT CALM IN THE WATER, AND WITH THE HELP OF THE GUIDE, FLIPPED THE BOAT BACK UP.
PUSHING AGAINST THE STRONG CURRENTS, I WADED OVER...
THE GUIDE AND EVERY KID DID THEIR BEST TO HOIST ME IN...
GO ON WITHOUT ME!

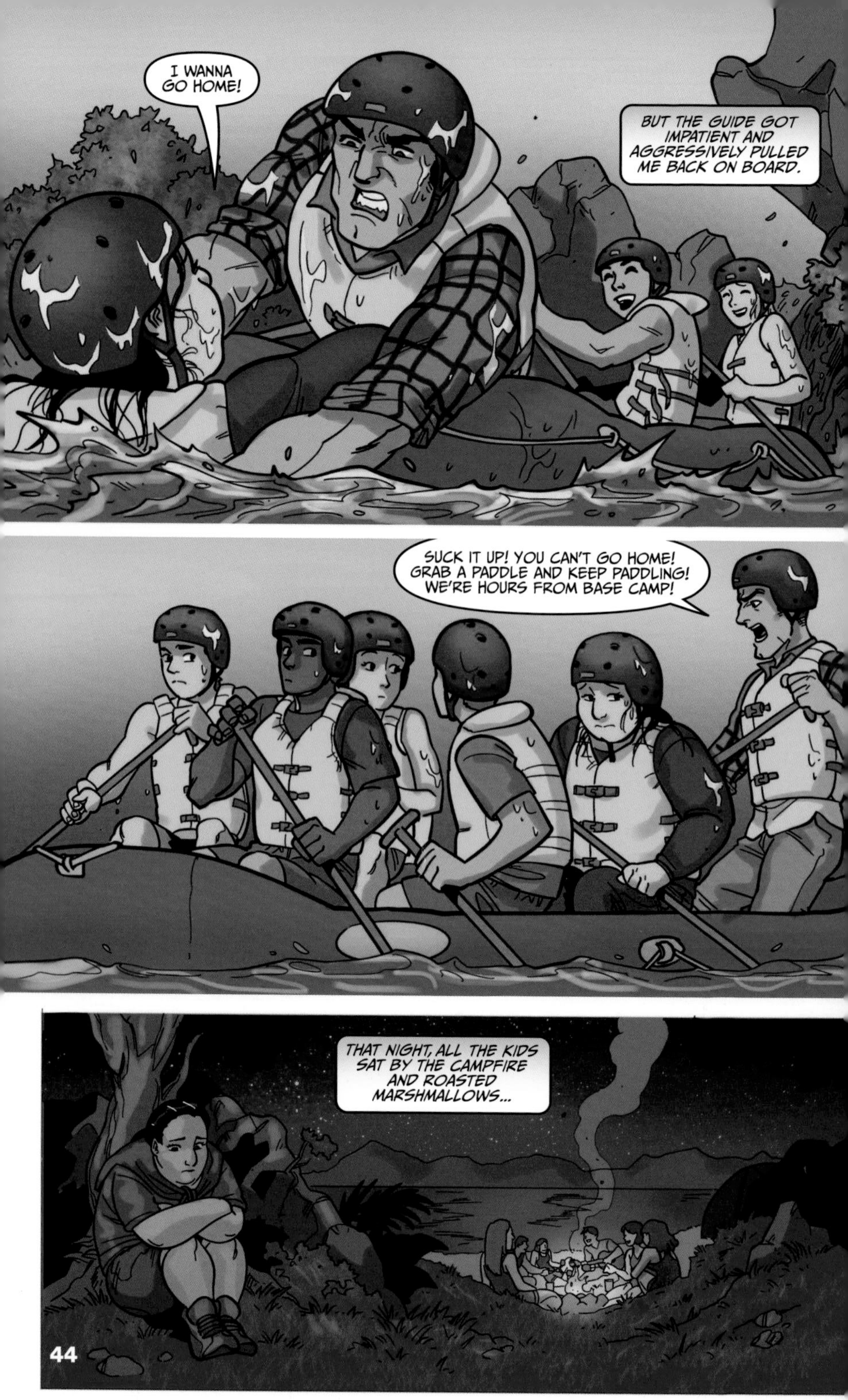

I WANNA GO HOME!
BUT THE GUIDE GOT IMPATIENT AND AGGRESSIVELY PULLED ME BACK ON BOARD.
SUCK IT UP! YOU CAN'T GO HOME! GRAB A PADDLE AND KEEP PADDLING! WE'RE HOURS FROM BASE CAMP!
THAT NIGHT, ALL THE KIDS SAT BY THE CAMPFIRE AND ROASTED MARSHMALLOWS...

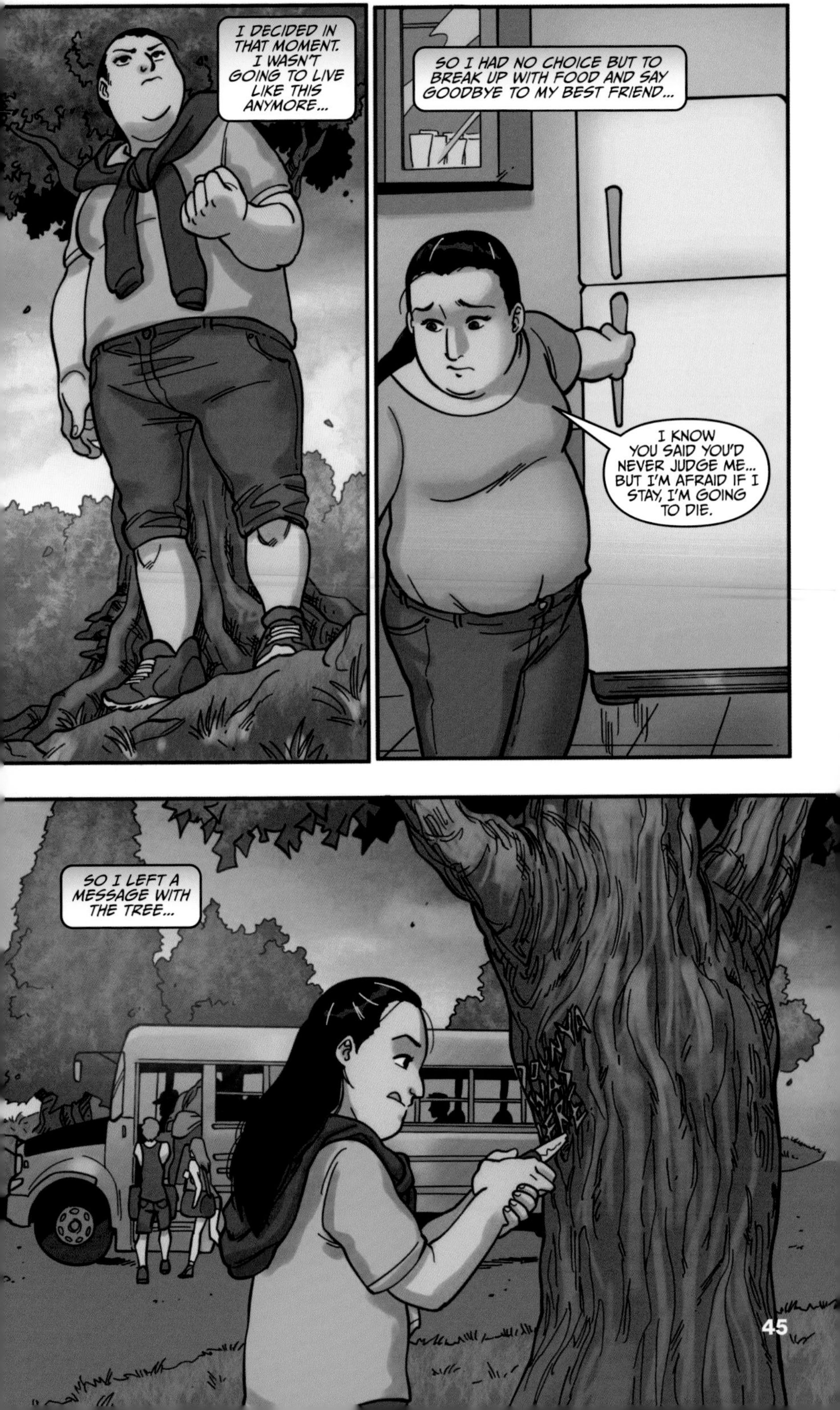
I DECIDED IN THAT MOMENT. I WASN'T GOING TO LIVE LIKE THIS ANYMORE...
SO I HAD NO CHOICE BUT TO BREAK UP WITH FOOD AND SAY GOODBYE TO MY BEST FRIEND...
I KNOW YOU SAID YOU'D NEVER JUDGE ME... BUT I'M AFRAID IF I STAY, I'M GOING TO DIE.
SO I LEFT A MESSAGE WITH THE TREE...

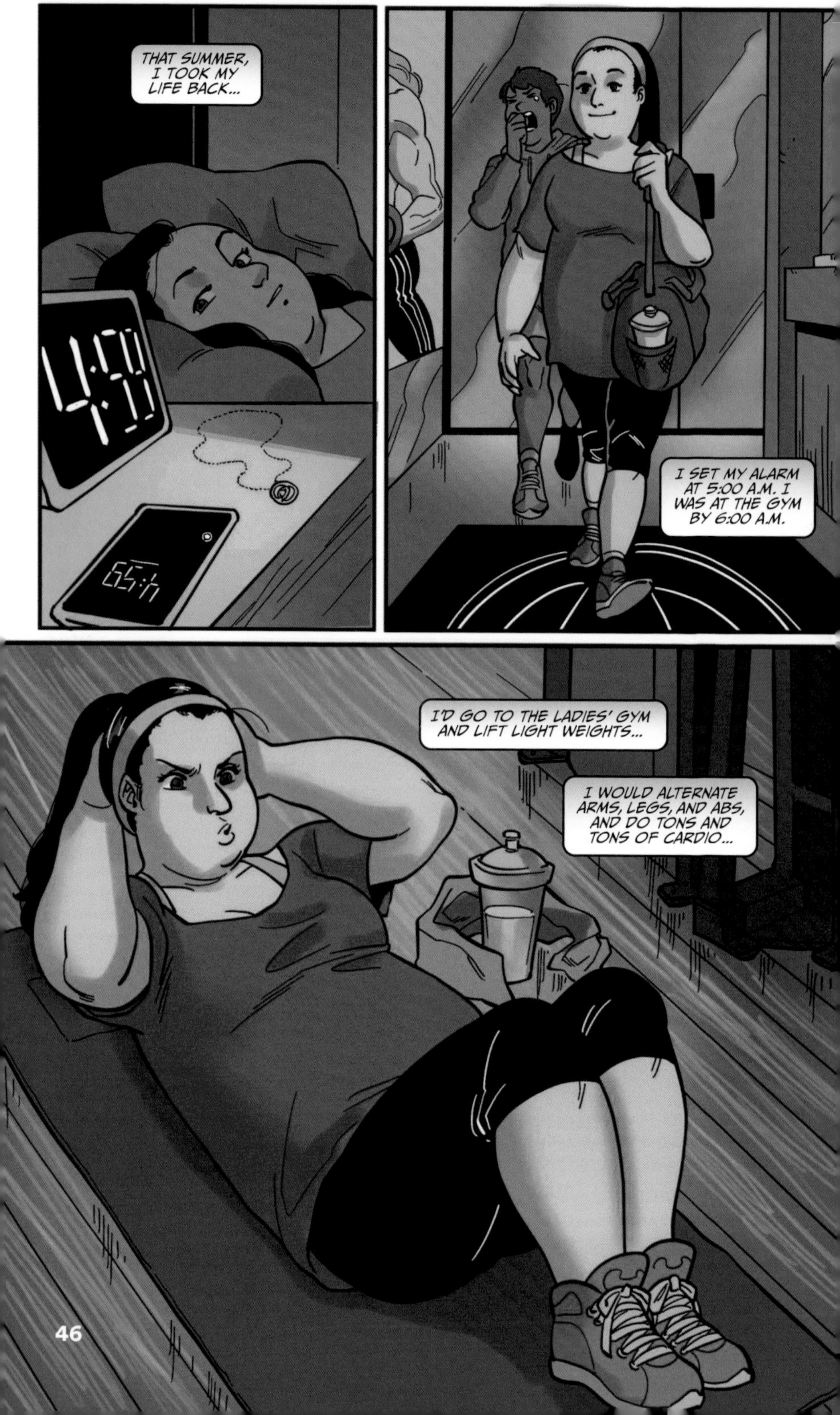
THAT SUMMER, I TOOK MY LIFE BACK...
I SET MY ALARM AT 5:00 A.M. I WAS AT THE GYM BY 6:00 A.M.
I'D GO TO THE LADIES' GYM AND LIFT LIGHT WEIGHTS...
I WOULD ALTERNATE ARMS, LEGS, AND ABS, AND DO TONS AND TONS OF CARDIO...

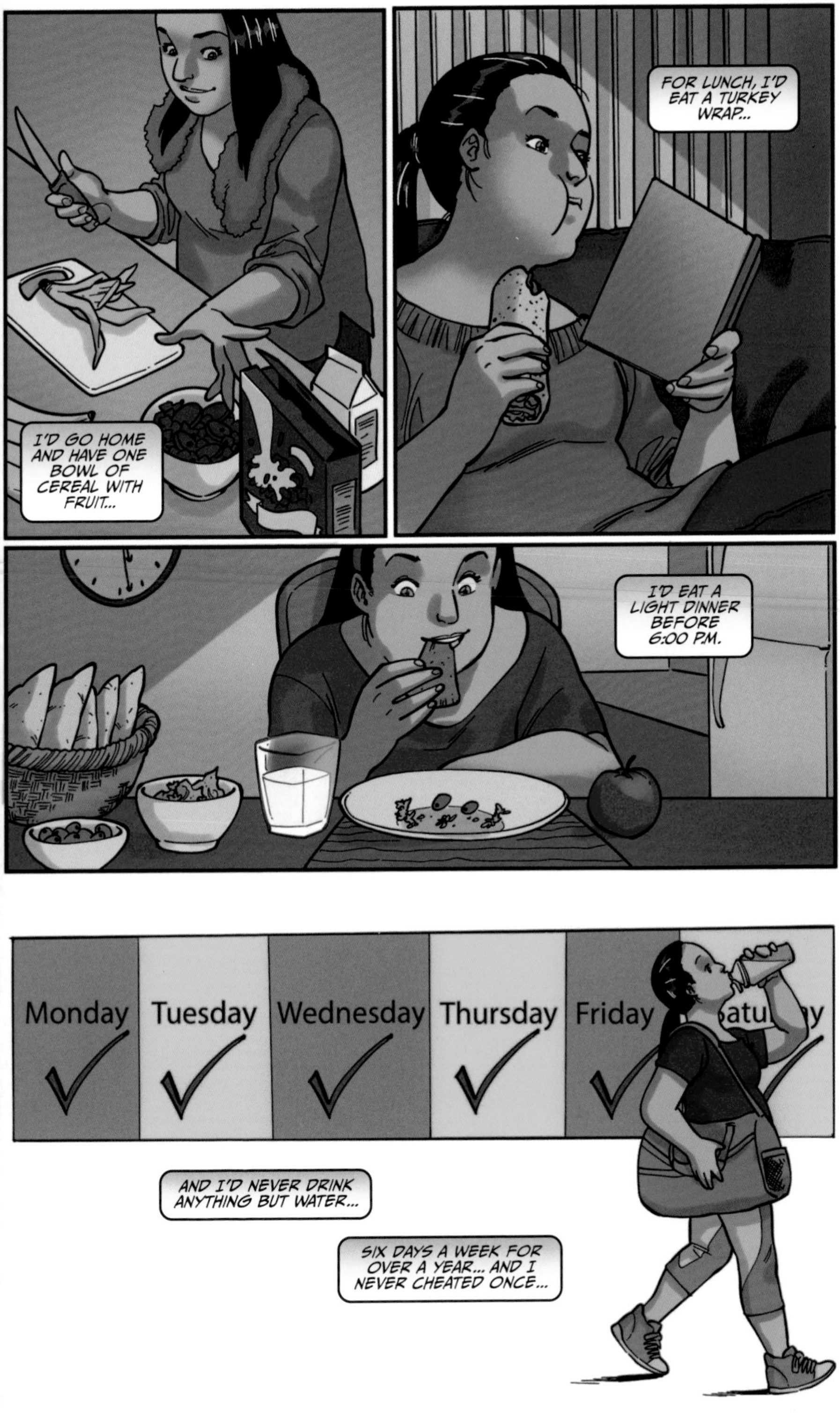
I'D GO HOME AND HAVE ONE BOWL OF CEREAL WITH FRUIT...
FOR LUNCH, I'D EAT A TURKEY WRAP...
I'D EAT A LIGHT DINNER BEFORE 6:00 P.M.
Monday
Tuesday
Wednesday
Thursday
Friday
AND I'D NEVER DRINK ANYTHING BUT WATER...
SIX DAYS A WEEK FOR OVER A YEAR... AND I NEVER CHEATED ONCE...

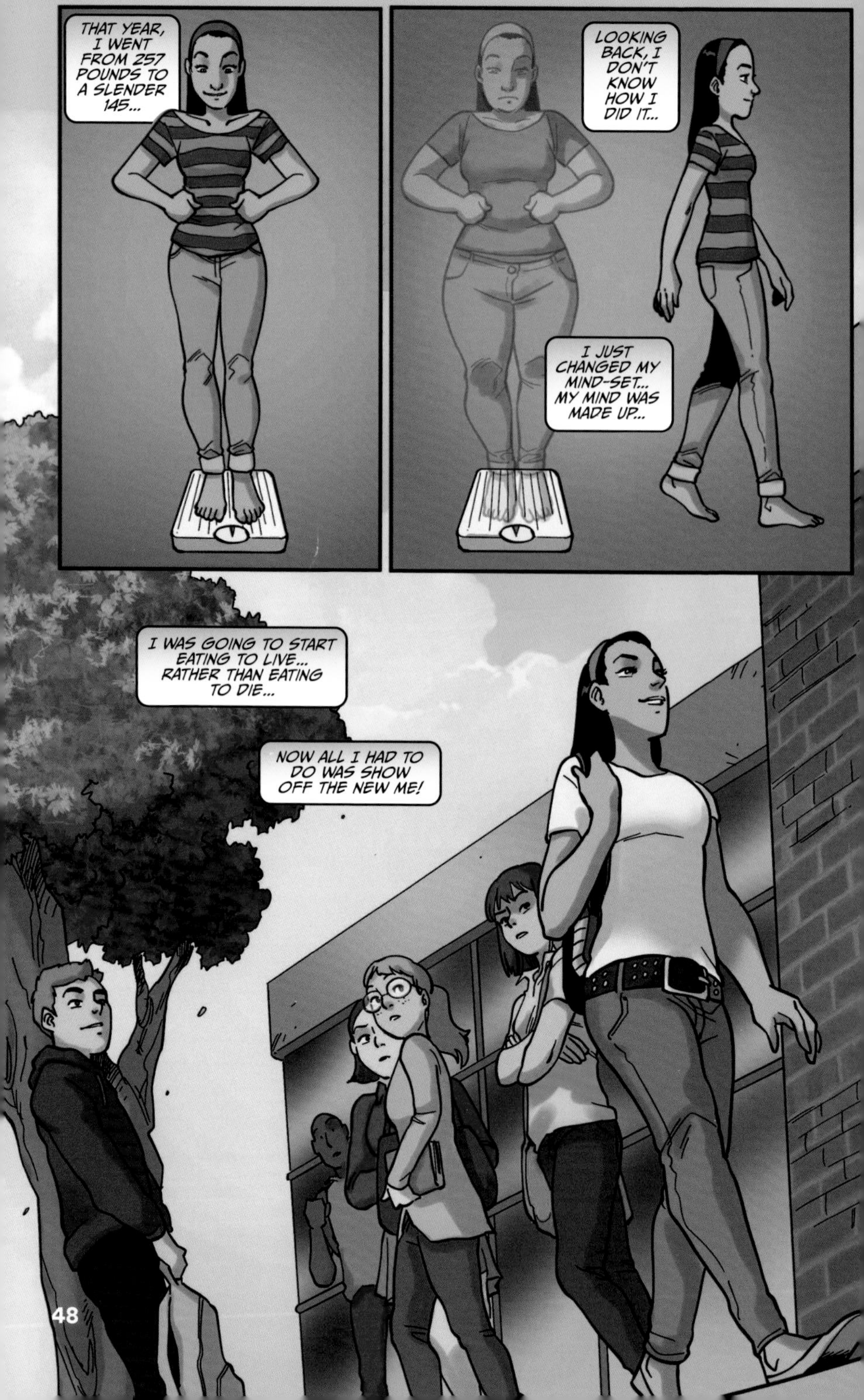
THAT YEAR, I WENT FROM 257 POUNDS TO A SLENDER 145...
LOOKING BACK, I DON'T KNOW HOW I DID IT...
I JUST CHANGED MY MIND-SET... MY MIND WAS MADE UP...
I WAS GOING TO START EATING TO LIVE... RATHER THAN EATING TO DIE...
NOW ALL I HAD TO DO WAS SHOW OFF THE NEW ME!

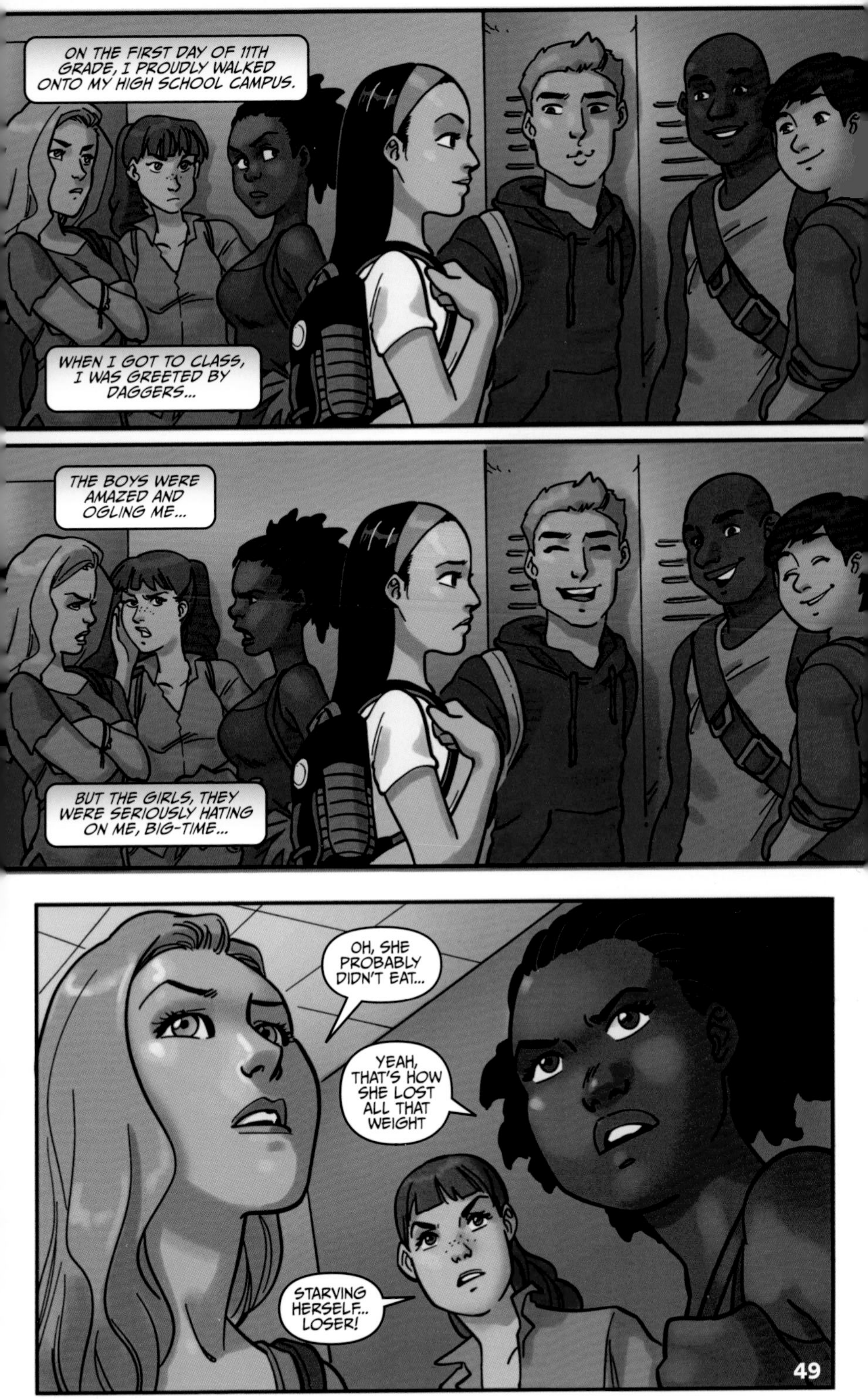
ON THE FIRST DAY OF 11TH GRADE, I PROUDLY WALKED ONTO MY HIGH SCHOOL CAMPUS.
WHEN I GOT TO CLASS, I WAS GREETED BY DAGGERS...
THE BOYS WERE AMAZED AND OGLING ME...
BUT THE GIRLS, THEY WERE SERIOUSLY HATING ON ME, BIG-TIME...
OH, SHE PROBABLY DIDN'T EAT...
YEAH, THAT'S HOW SHE LOST ALL THAT WEIGHT
STARVING HERSELF... LOSER!

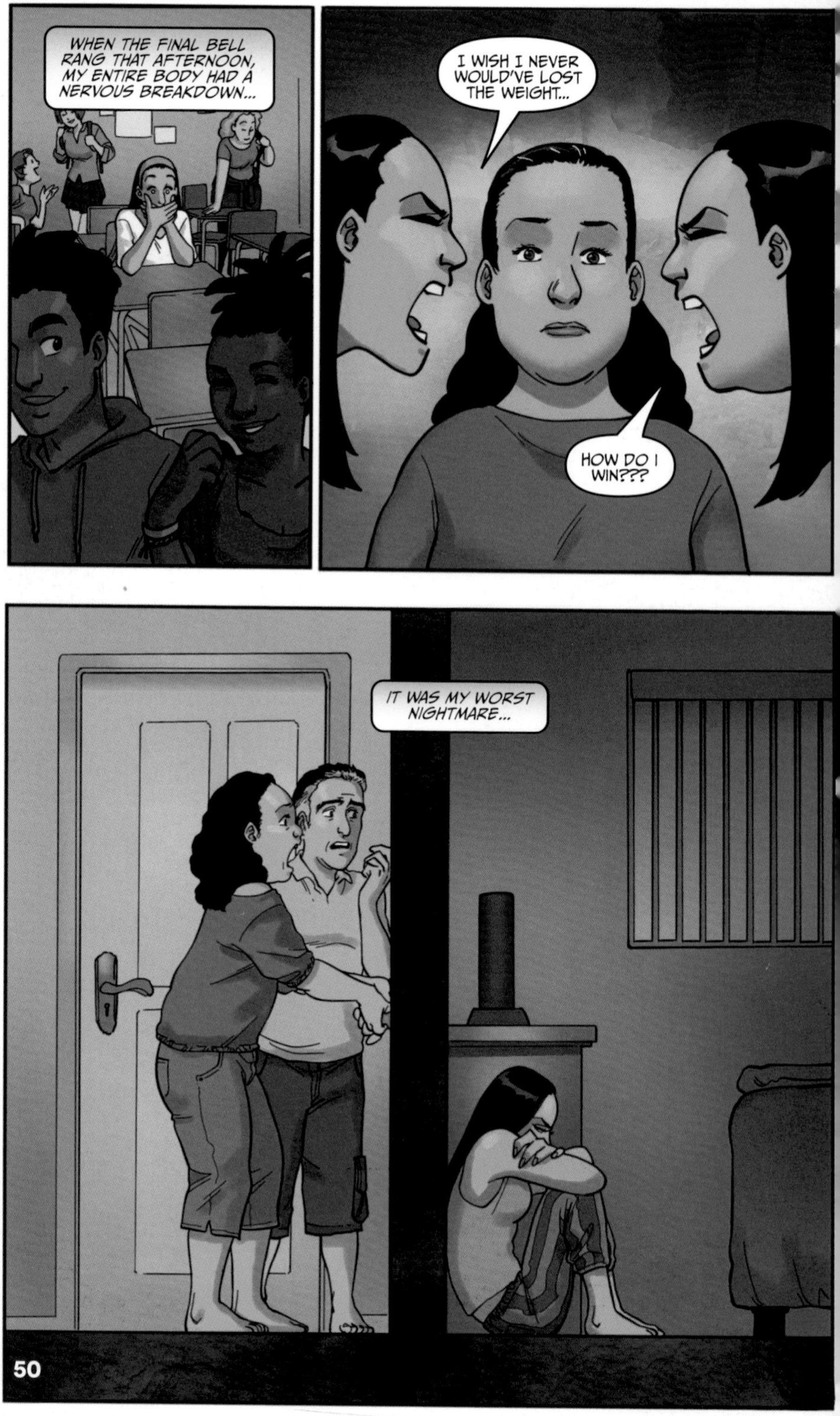
WHEN THE FINAL BELL RANG THAT AFTERNOON, MY ENTIRE BODY HAD A NERVOUS BREAKDOWN...
I WISH I NEVER WOULD'VE LOST THE WEIGHT...
HOW DO I WIN???
IT WAS MY WORST NIGHTMARE...

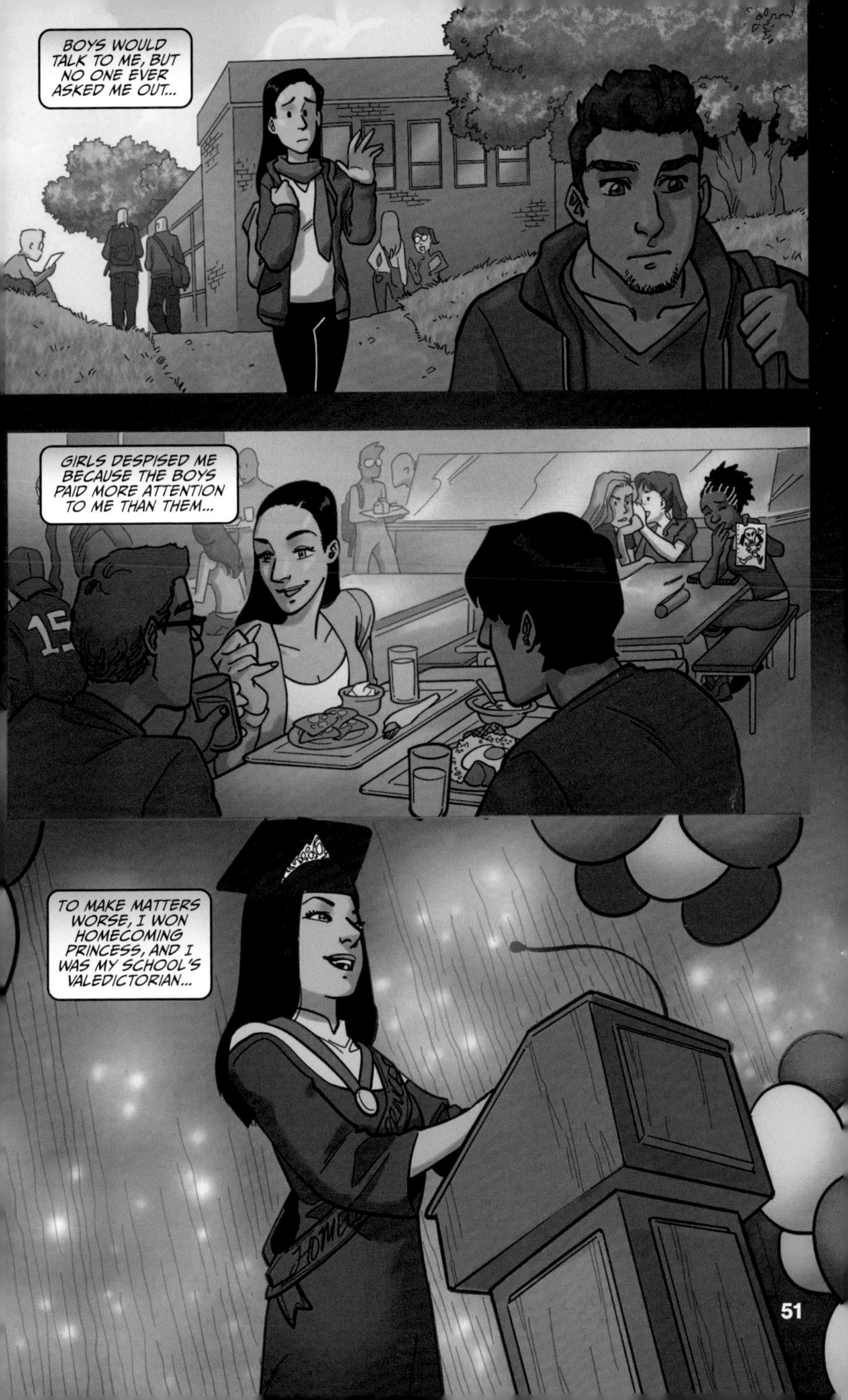

BOYS WOULD TALK TO ME, BUT NO ONE EVER ASKED ME OUT...
GIRLS DESPISED ME BECAUSE THE BOYS PAID MORE ATTENTION TO ME THAN THEM...
15
TO MAKE MATTERS WORSE, I WON HOMECOMING PRINCESS, AND I WAS MY SCHOOL'S VALEDICTORIAN...

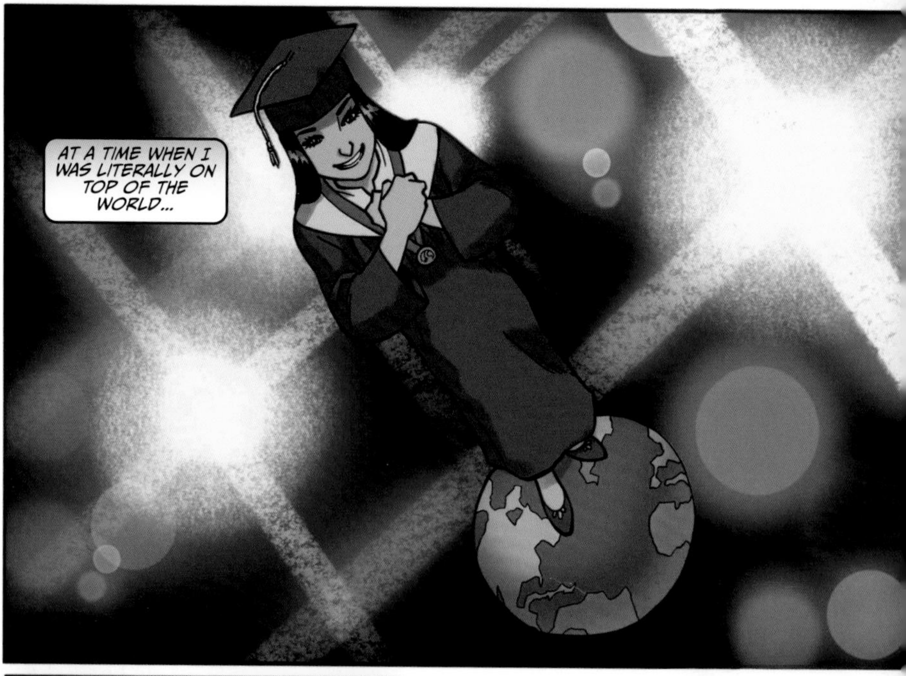
AT A TIME WHEN I WAS LITERALLY ON TOP OF THE WORLD...

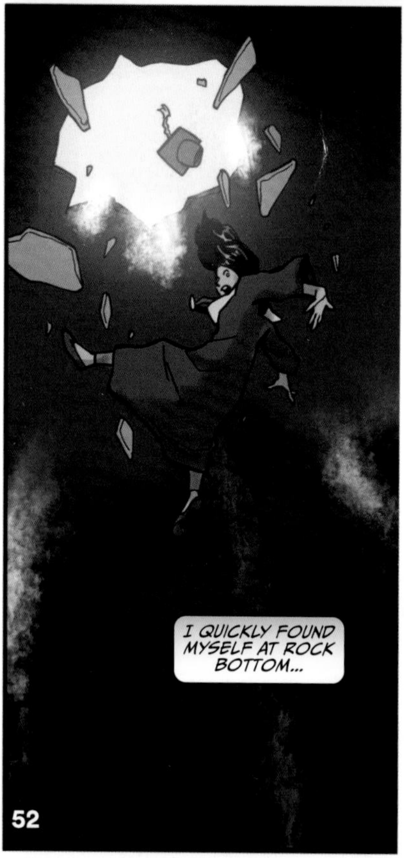
I QUICKLY FOUND MYSELF AT ROCK BOTTOM...

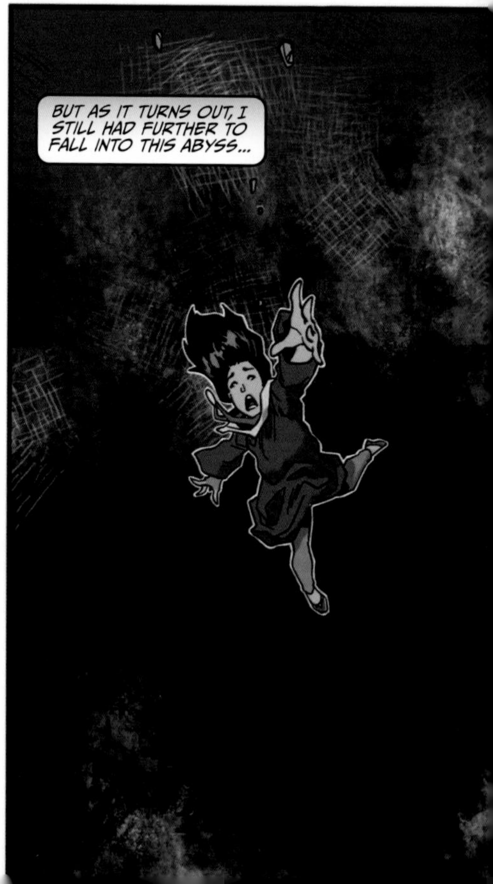
BUT AS IT TURNS OUT, I STILL HAD FURTHER TO FALL INTO THIS ABYSS...

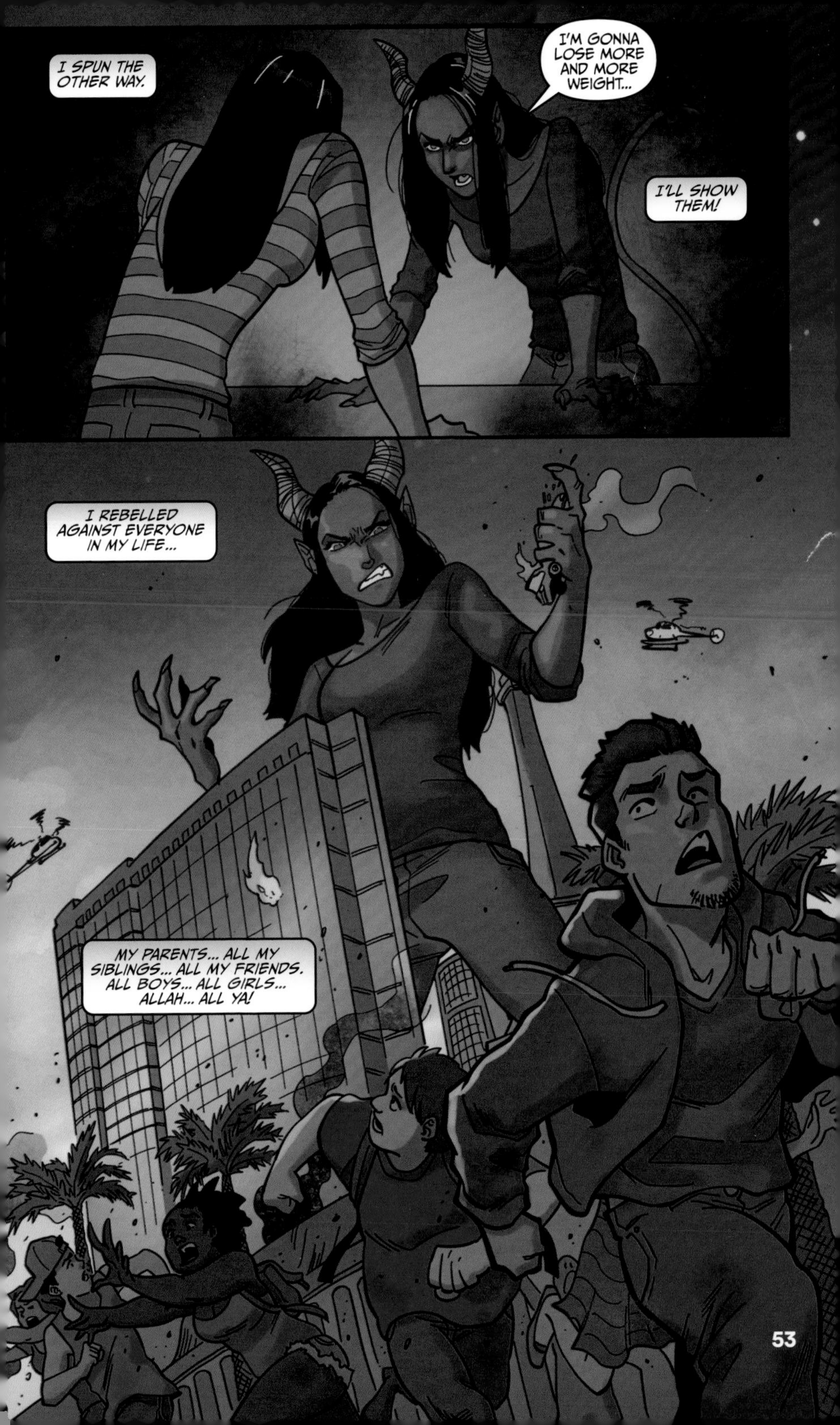
I SPUN THE OTHER WAY.
I'M GONNA LOSE MORE AND MORE WEIGHT...
I'LL SHOW THEM!
I REBELLED AGAINST EVERYONE IN MY LIFE...
MY PARENTS... ALL MY SIBLINGS... ALL MY FRIENDS. ALL BOYS... ALL GIRLS... ALLAH... ALL YA!

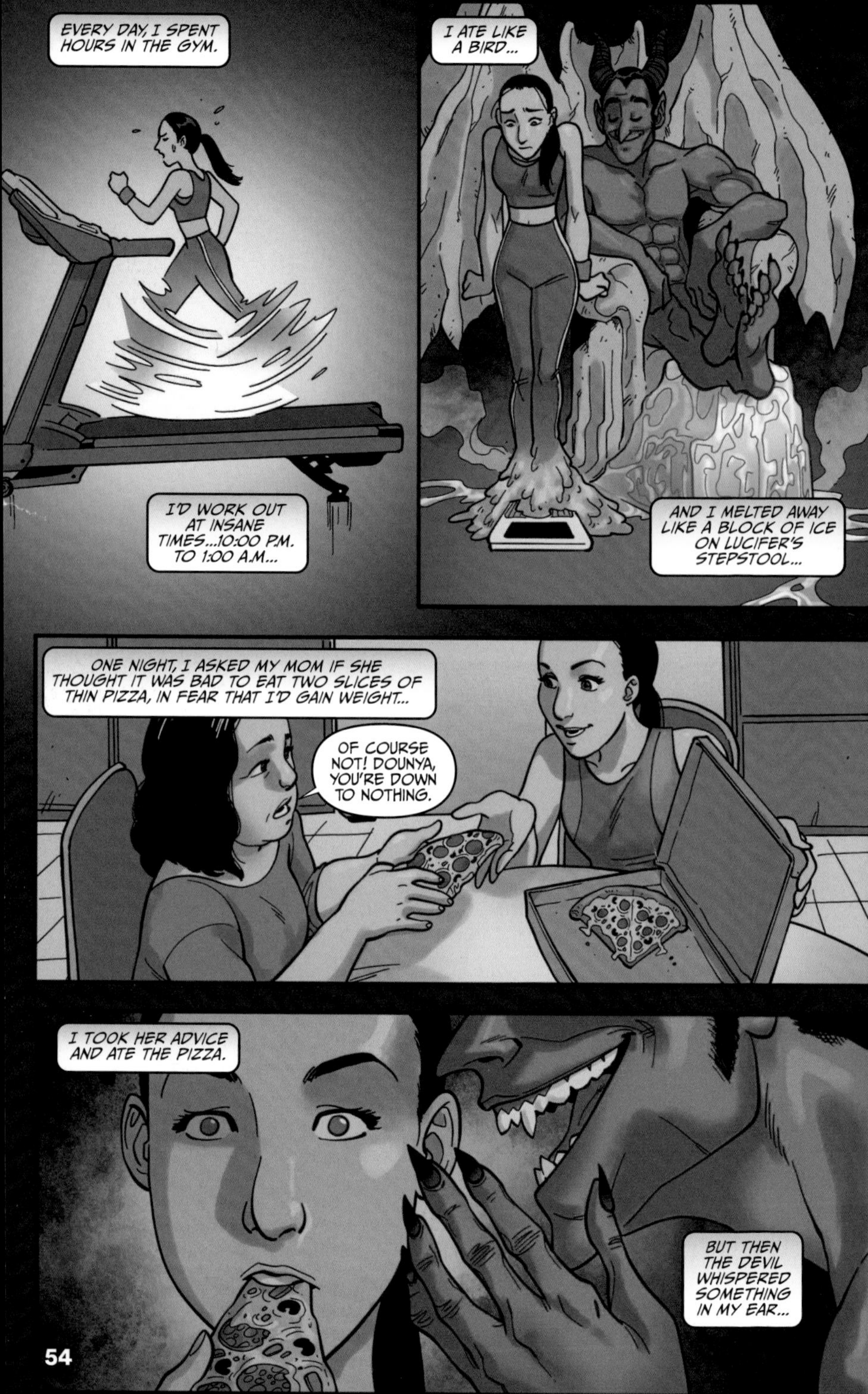
EVERY DAY, I SPENT HOURS IN THE GYM.
I'D WORK OUT AT INSANE TIMES...10:00 P.M. TO 1:00 A.M...
I ATE LIKE A BIRD...
AND I MELTED AWAY LIKE A BLOCK OF ICE ON LUCIFER'S STEPSTOOL...
ONE NIGHT, I ASKED MY MOM IF SHE THOUGHT IT WAS BAD TO EAT TWO SLICES OF THIN PIZZA, IN FEAR THAT I'D GAIN WEIGHT...
OF COURSE NOT! DOUNYA, YOU'RE DOWN TO NOTHING.
I TOOK HER ADVICE AND ATE THE PIZZA.
BUT THEN THE DEVIL WHISPERED SOMETHING IN MY EAR...

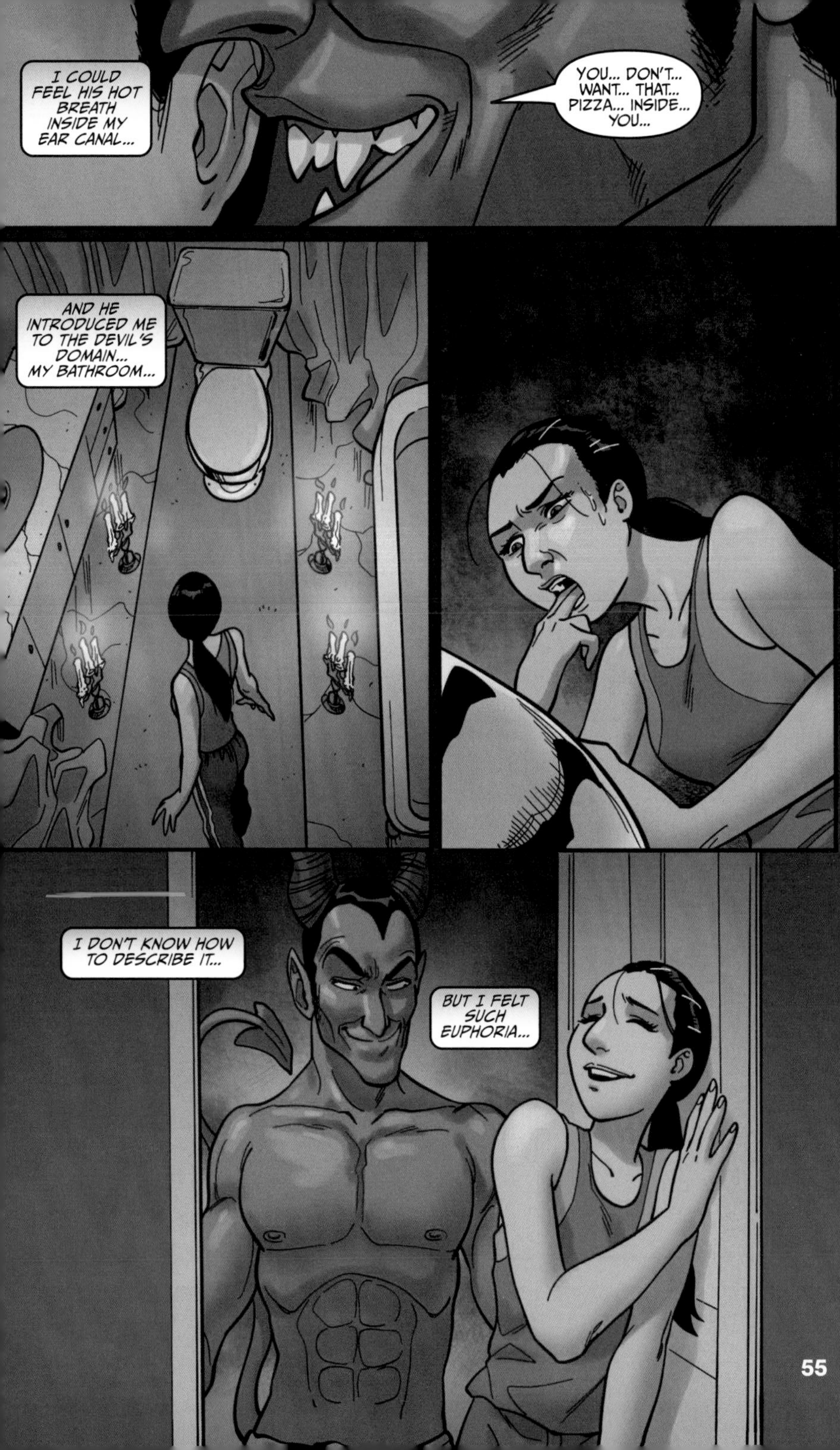
I COULD FEEL HIS HOT BREATH INSIDE MY EAR CANAL...
YOU... DON'T... WANT... THAT... PIZZA... INSIDE... YOU...
AND HE INTRODUCED ME TO THE DEVIL'S DOMAIN... MY BATHROOM...
I DON'T KNOW HOW TO DESCRIBE IT...
BUT I FELT SUCH EUPHORIA...

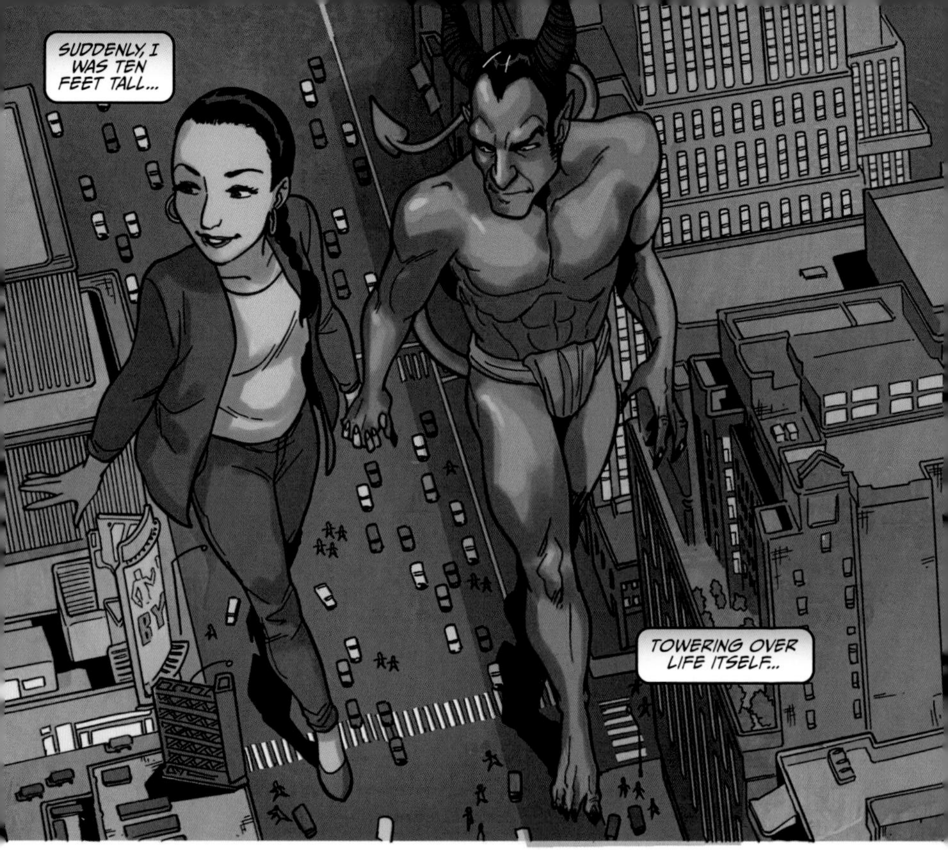
SUDDENLY, I WAS TEN FEET TALL...
TOWERING OVER LIFE ITSELF...
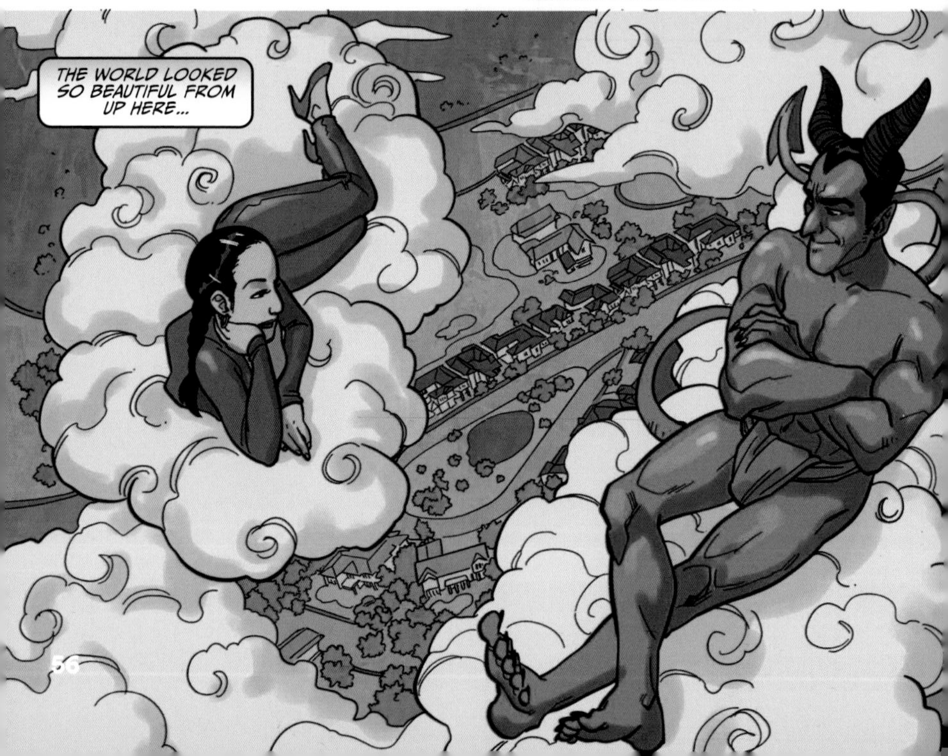
THE WORLD LOOKED SO BEAUTIFUL FROM UP HERE...

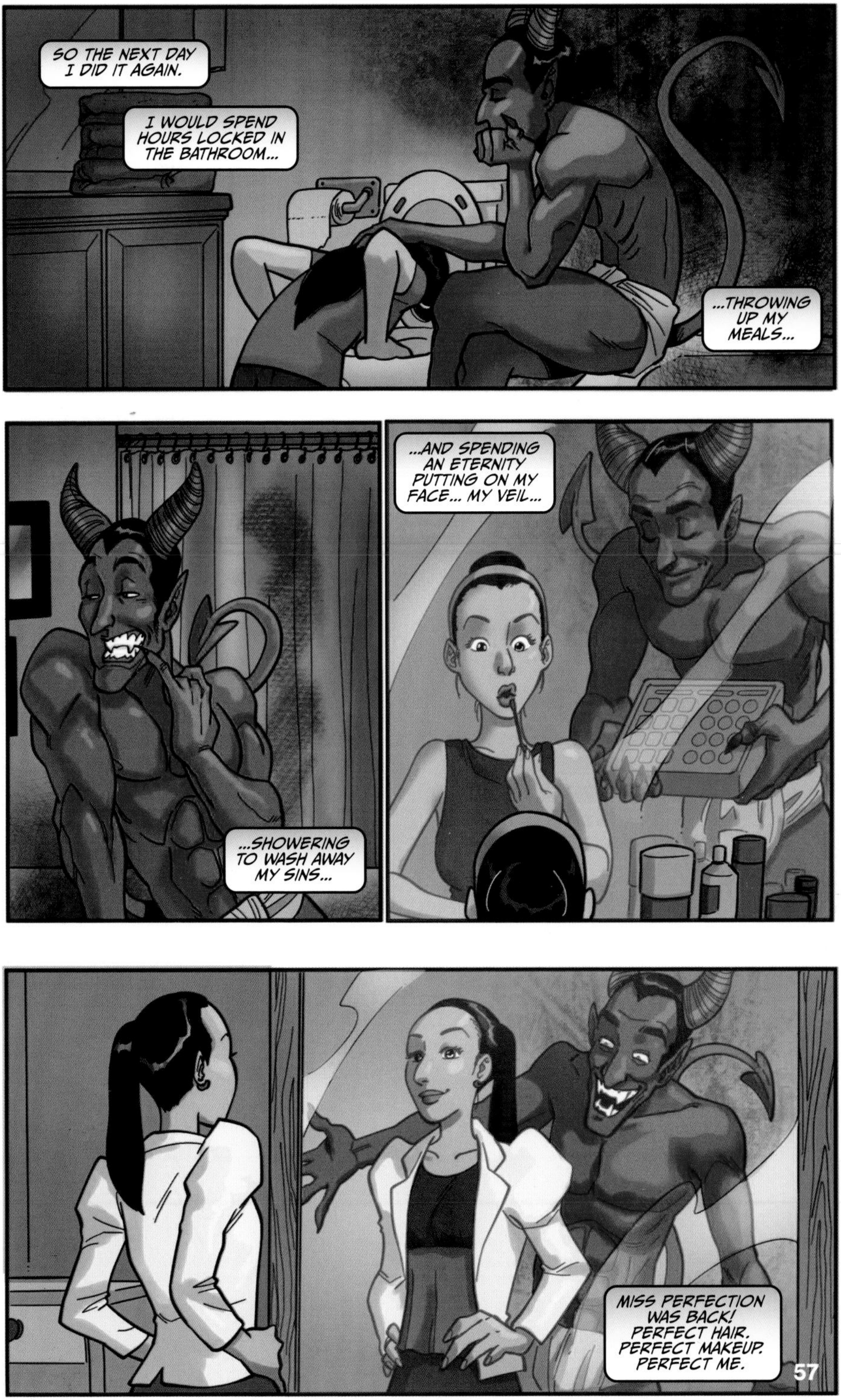
SO THE NEXT DAY I DID IT AGAIN.
I WOULD SPEND HOURS LOCKED IN THE BATHROOM...
...THROWING UP MY MEALS...
...SHOWERING TO WASH AWAY MY SINS...
...AND SPENDING AN ETERNITY PUTTING ON MY FACE... MY VEIL...
MISS PERFECTION WAS BACK! PERFECT HAIR. PERFECT MAKEUP. PERFECT ME.

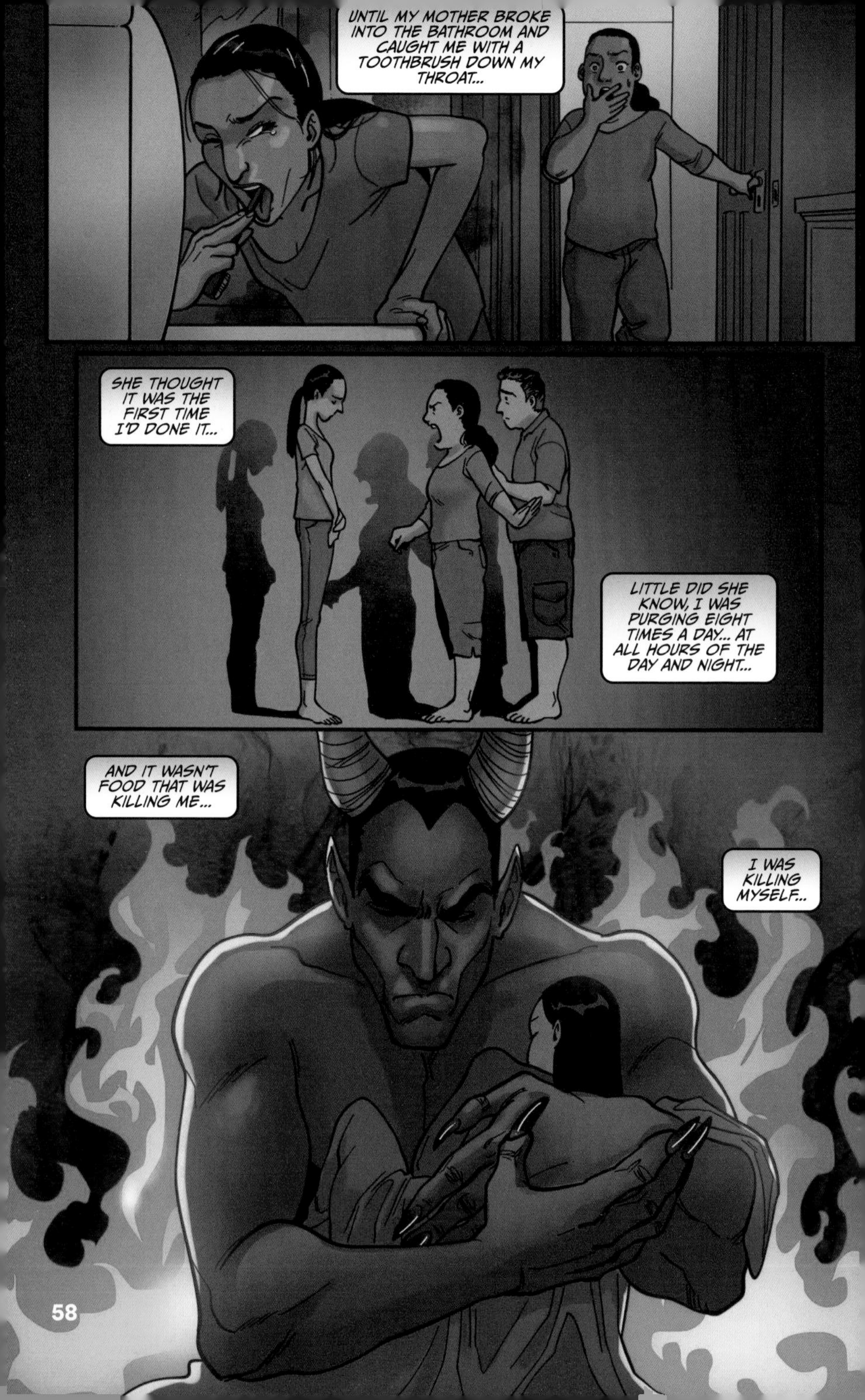
UNTIL MY MOTHER BROKE INTO THE BATHROOM AND CAUGHT ME WITH A TOOTHBRUSH DOWN MY THROAT...
SHE THOUGHT IT WAS THE FIRST TIME I'D DONE IT...
LITTLE DID SHE KNOW, I WAS PURGING EIGHT TIMES A DAY... AT ALL HOURS OF THE DAY AND NIGHT...
AND IT WASN'T FOOD THAT WAS KILLING ME...
I WAS KILLING MYSELF...

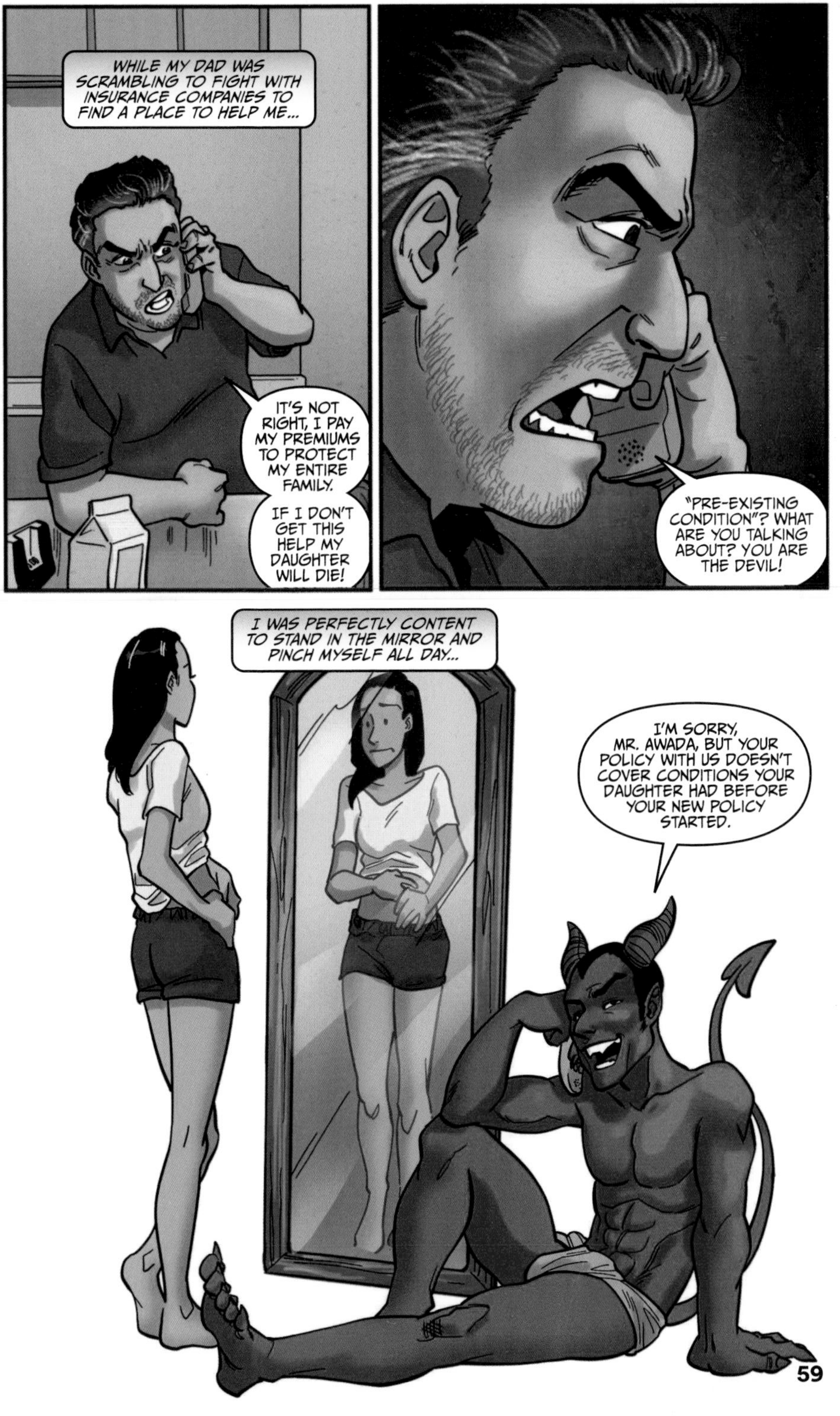
WHILE MY DAD WAS SCRAMBLING TO FIGHT WITH INSURANCE COMPANIES TO FIND A PLACE TO HELP ME...
IT'S NOT RIGHT, I PAY MY PREMIUMS TO PROTECT MY ENTIRE FAMILY.
IF I DON'T GET THIS HELP MY DAUGHTER WILL DIE!
"PRE-EXISTING CONDITION"? WHAT ARE YOU TALKING ABOUT? YOU ARE THE DEVIL!
I WAS PERFECTLY CONTENT TO STAND IN THE MIRROR AND PINCH MYSELF ALL DAY...
I'M SORRY, MR. AWADA, BUT YOUR POLICY WITH US DOESN'T COVER CONDITIONS YOUR DAUGHTER HAD BEFORE YOUR NEW POLICY STARTED.

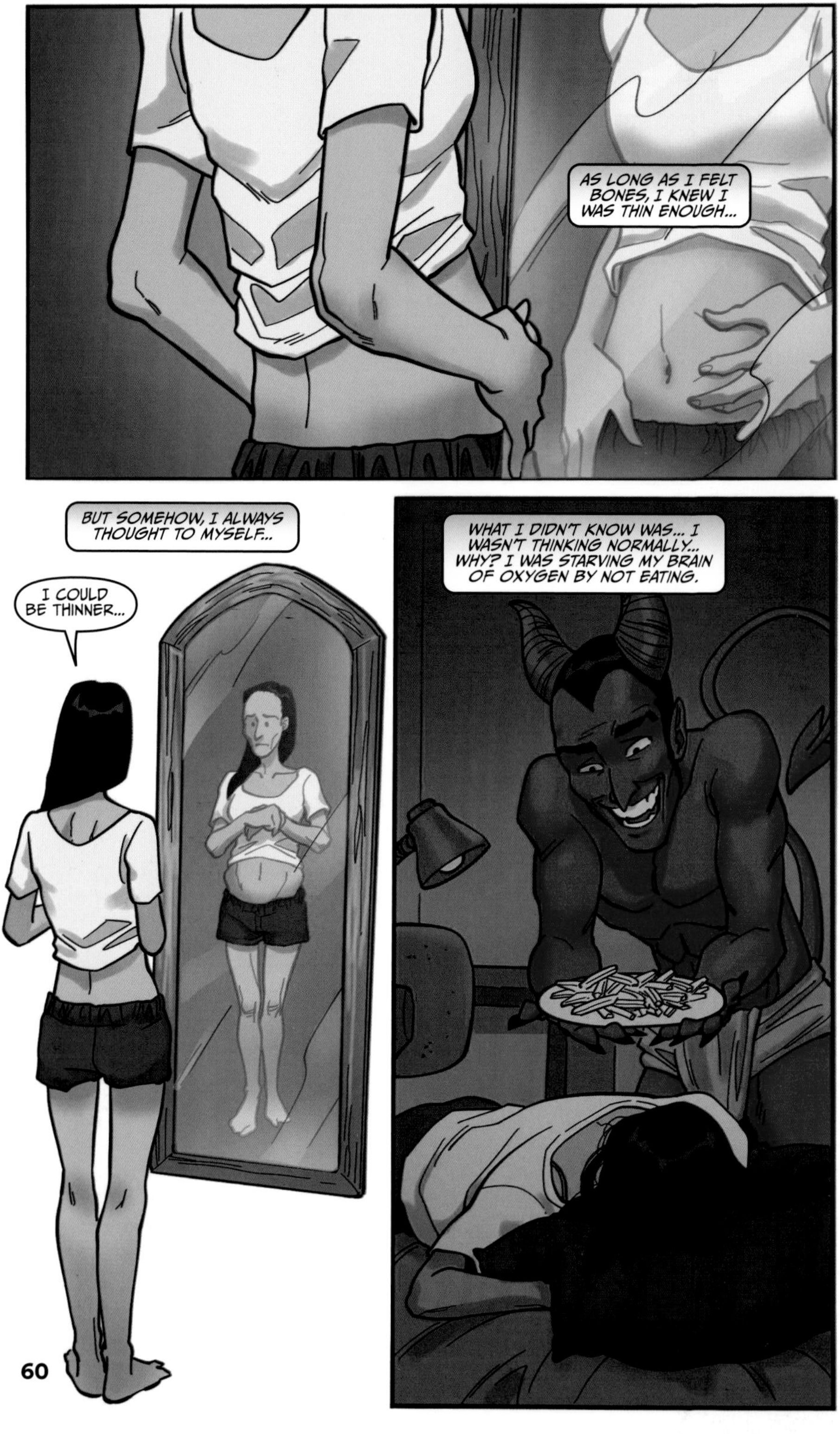
AS LONG AS I FELT BONES, I KNEW I WAS THIN ENOUGH...
BUT SOMEHOW, I ALWAYS THOUGHT TO MYSELF...
I COULD BE THINNER...
WHAT I DIDN'T KNOW WAS... I WASN'T THINKING NORMALLY... WHY? I WAS STARVING MY BRAIN OF OXYGEN BY NOT EATING.

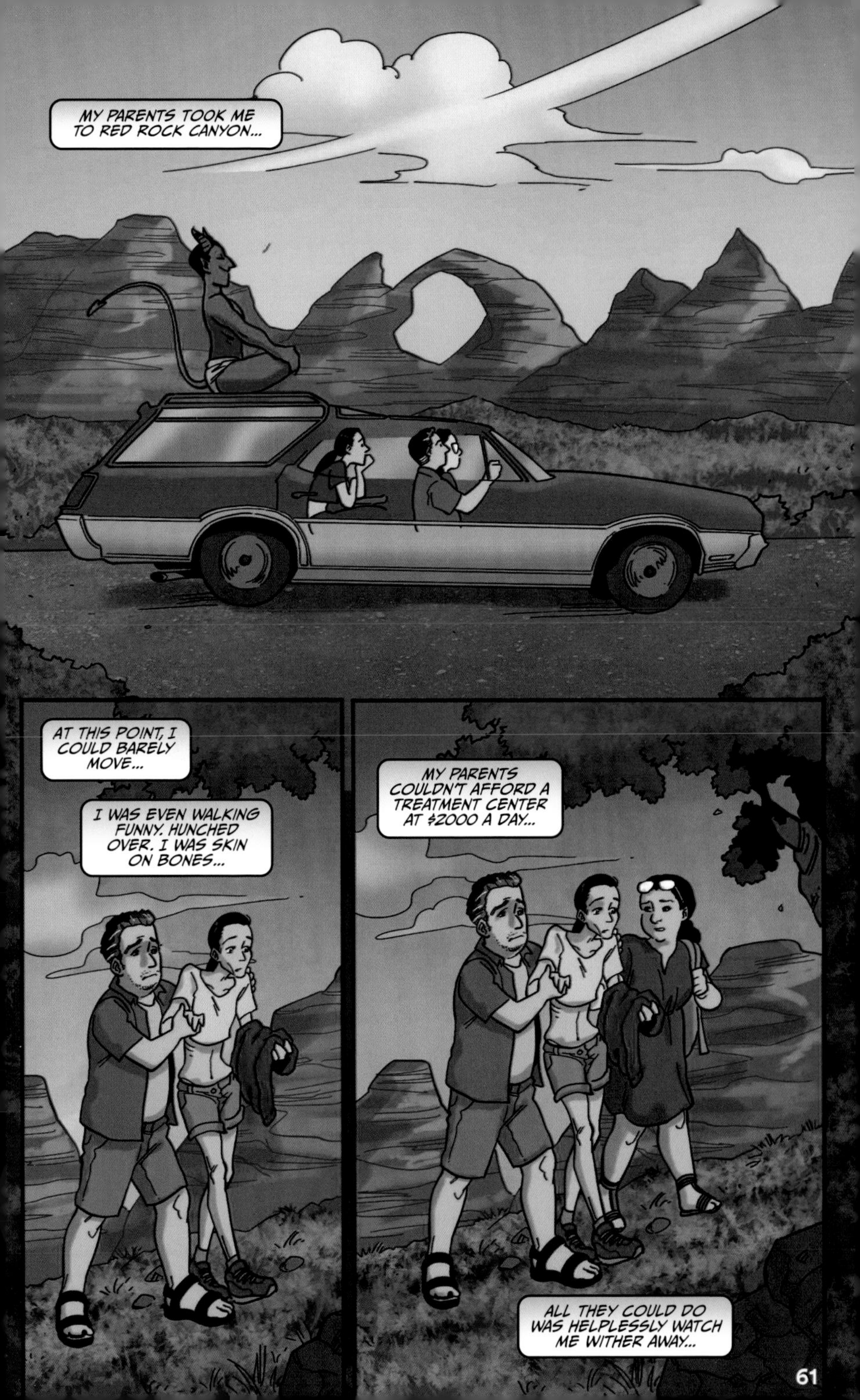
MY PARENTS TOOK ME TO RED ROCK CANYON...
AT THIS POINT, I COULD BARELY MOVE...
I WAS EVEN WALKING FUNNY. HUNCHED OVER. I WAS SKIN ON BONES...
MY PARENTS COULDN'T AFFORD A TREATMENT CENTER AT $2000 A DAY...
ALL THEY COULD DO WAS HELPLESSLY WATCH ME WITHER AWAY...

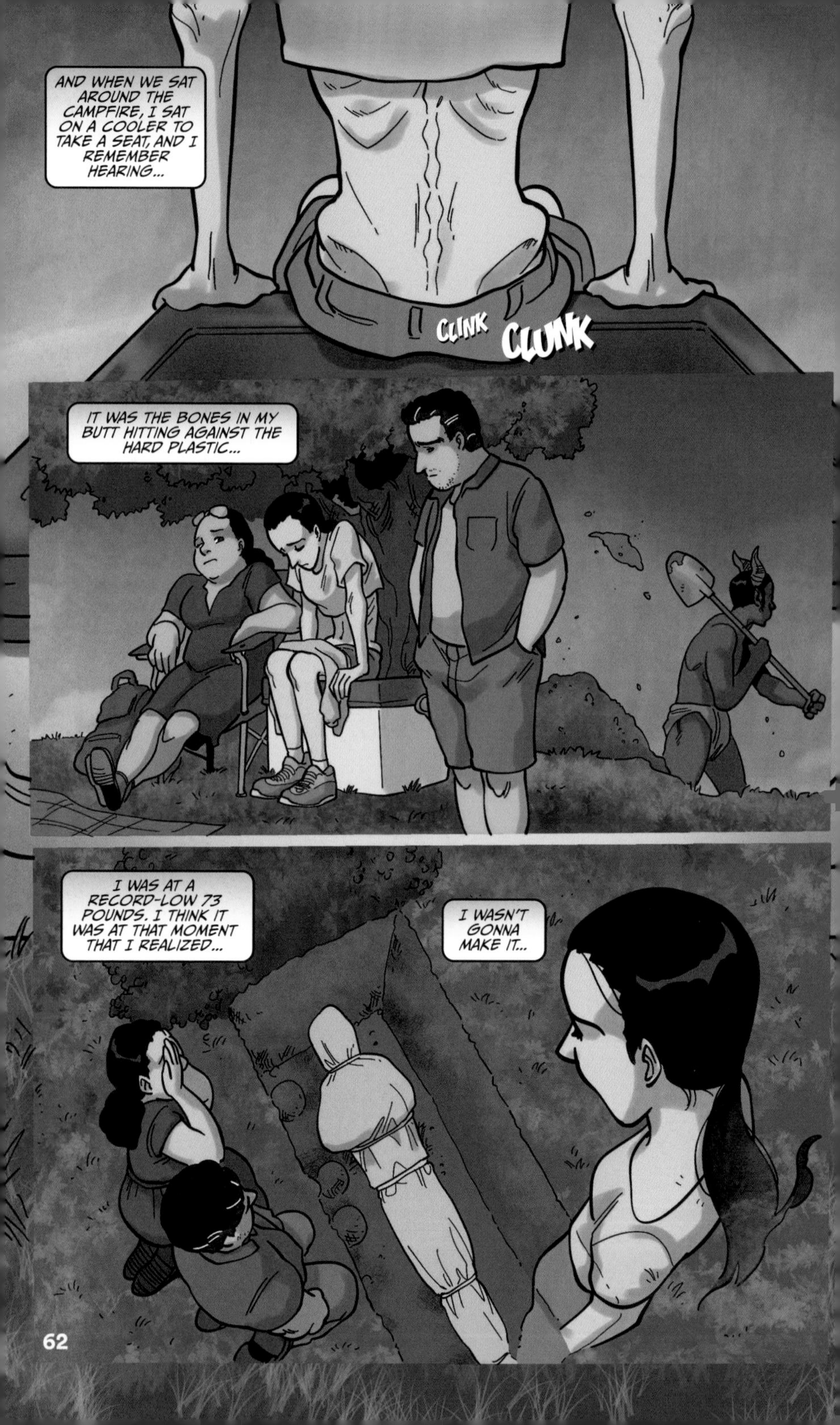
AND WHEN WE SAT AROUND THE CAMPFIRE, I SAT ON A COOLER TO TAKE A SEAT, AND I REMEMBER HEARING...
CLINK
CLUNK
IT WAS THE BONES IN MY BUTT HITTING AGAINST THE HARD PLASTIC...
I WAS AT A RECORD-LOW 73 POUNDS. I THINK IT WAS AT THAT MOMENT THAT I REALIZED...
I WASN'T GONNA MAKE IT...

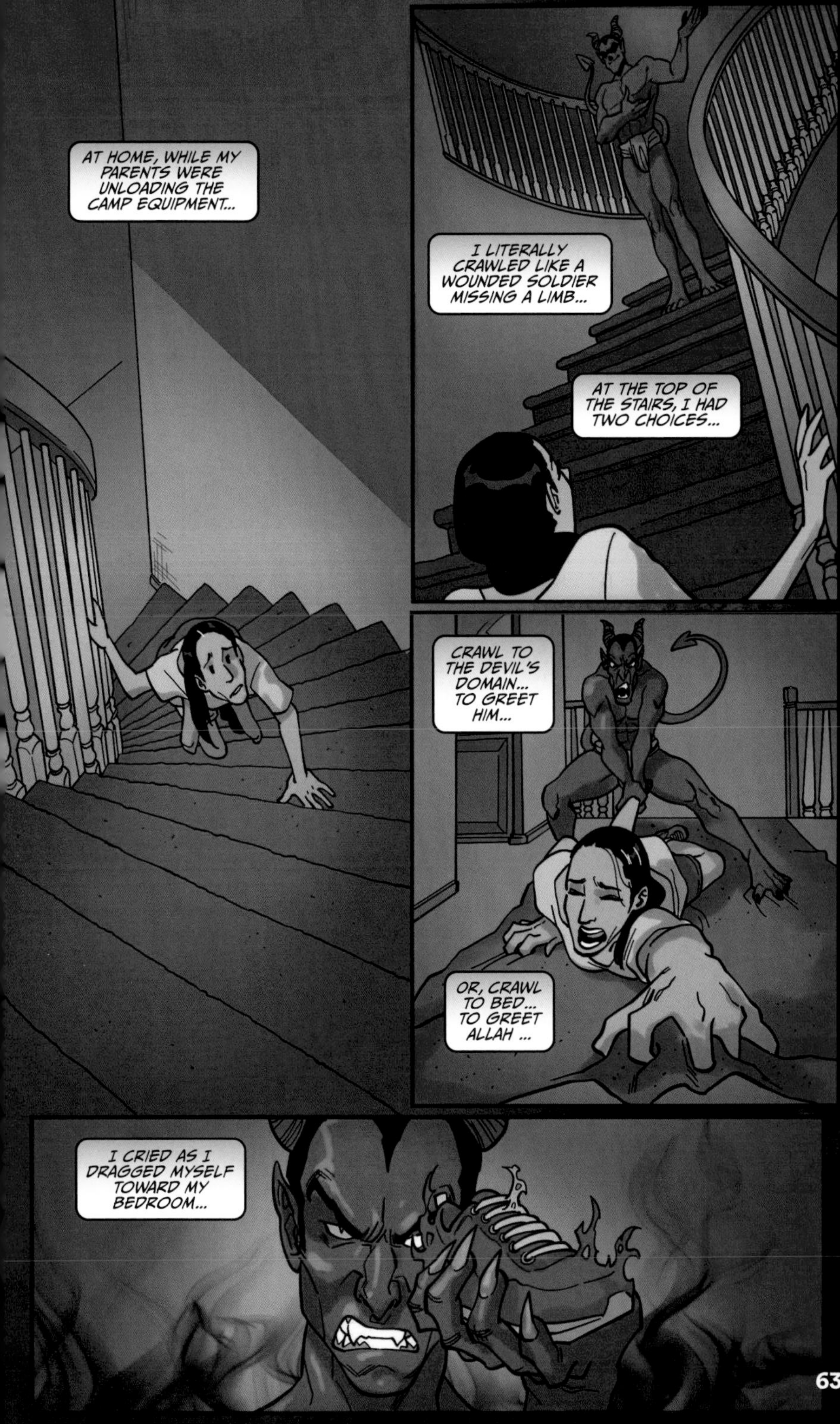
AT HOME, WHILE MY PARENTS WERE UNLOADING THE CAMP EQUIPMENT...
I LITERALLY CRAWLED LIKE A WOUNDED SOLDIER MISSING A LIMB...
AT THE TOP OF THE STAIRS, I HAD TWO CHOICES...
CRAWL TO THE DEVIL'S DOMAIN... TO GREET HIM...
OR, CRAWL TO BED... TO GREET ALLAH ...
I CRIED AS I DRAGGED MYSELF TOWARD MY BEDROOM...

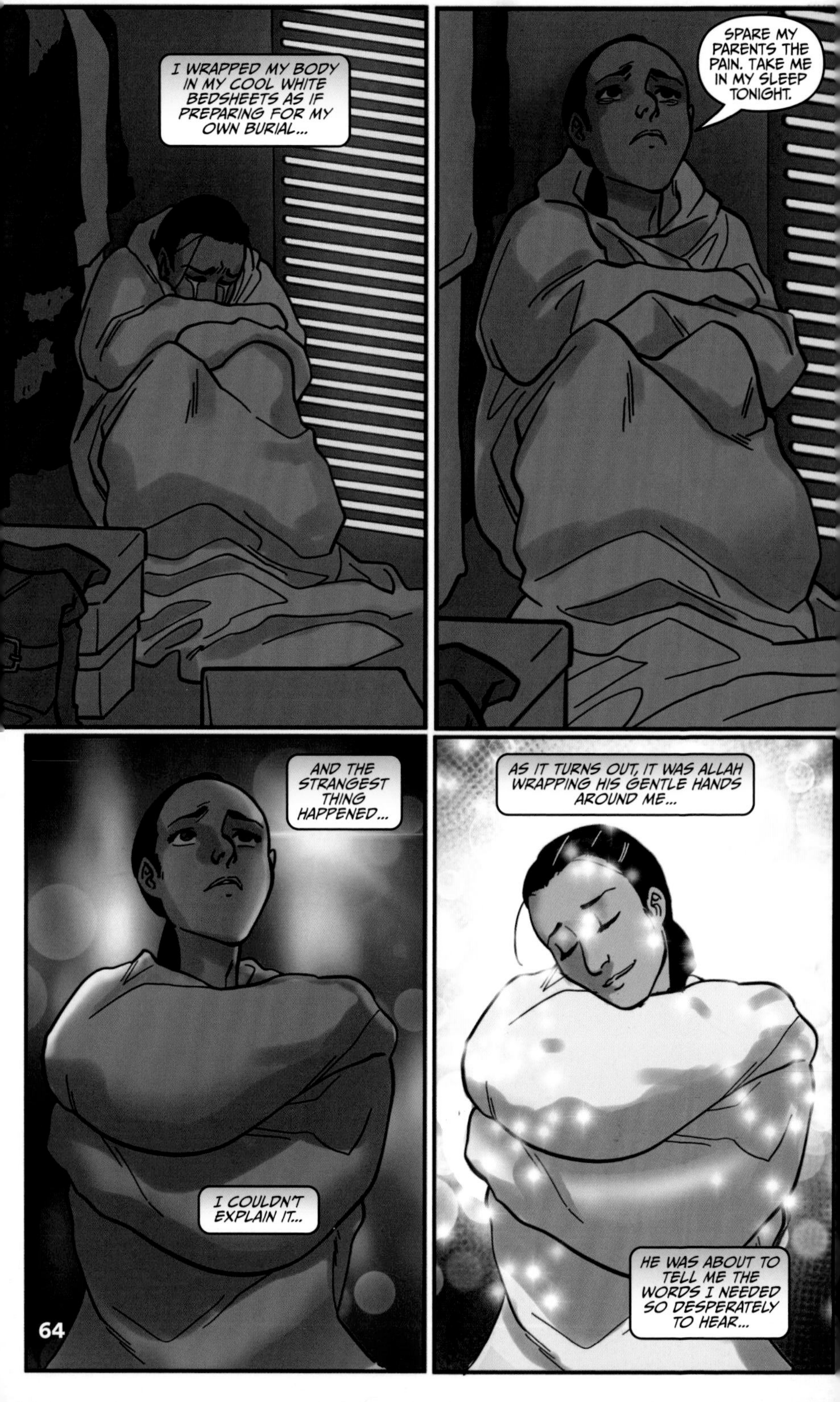

I WRAPPED MY BODY IN MY COOL WHITE BEDSHEETS AS IF PREPARING FOR MY OWN BURIAL...
SPARE MY PARENTS THE PAIN. TAKE ME IN MY SLEEP TONIGHT.
AND THE STRANGEST THING HAPPENED...
I COULDN'T EXPLAIN IT...
AS IT TURNS OUT, IT WAS ALLAH WRAPPING HIS GENTLE HANDS AROUND ME...
HE WAS ABOUT TO TELL ME THE WORDS I NEEDED SO DESPERATELY TO HEAR...

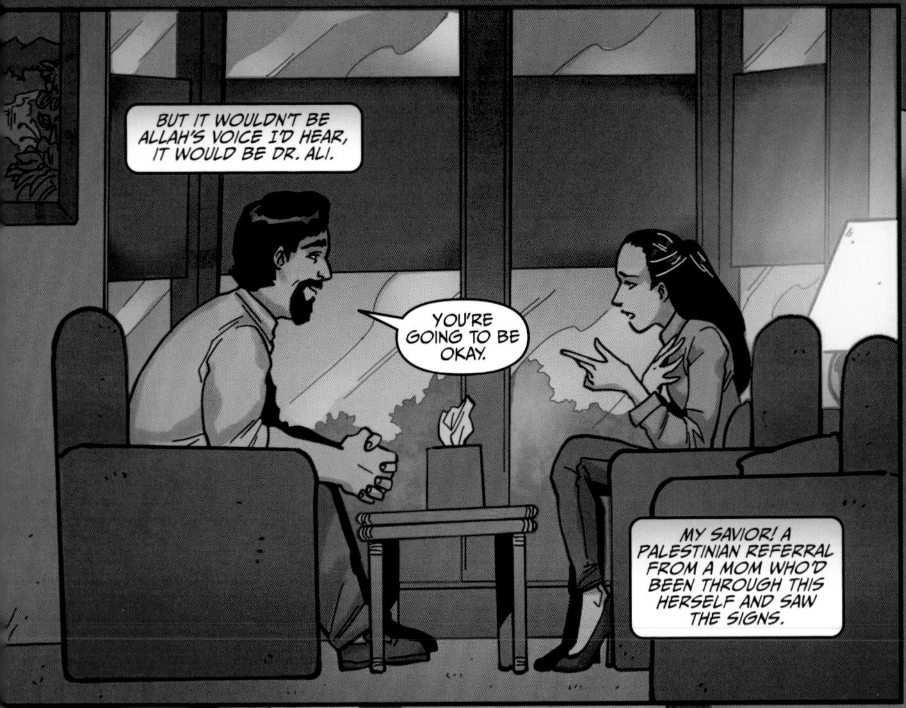
BUT IT WOULDN'T BE ALLAH'S VOICE I'D HEAR, IT WOULD BE DR. ALI.
YOU'RE GOING TO BE OKAY.
MY SAVIOR! A PALESTINIAN REFERRAL FROM A MOM WHO'D BEEN THROUGH THIS HERSELF AND SAW THE SIGNS.

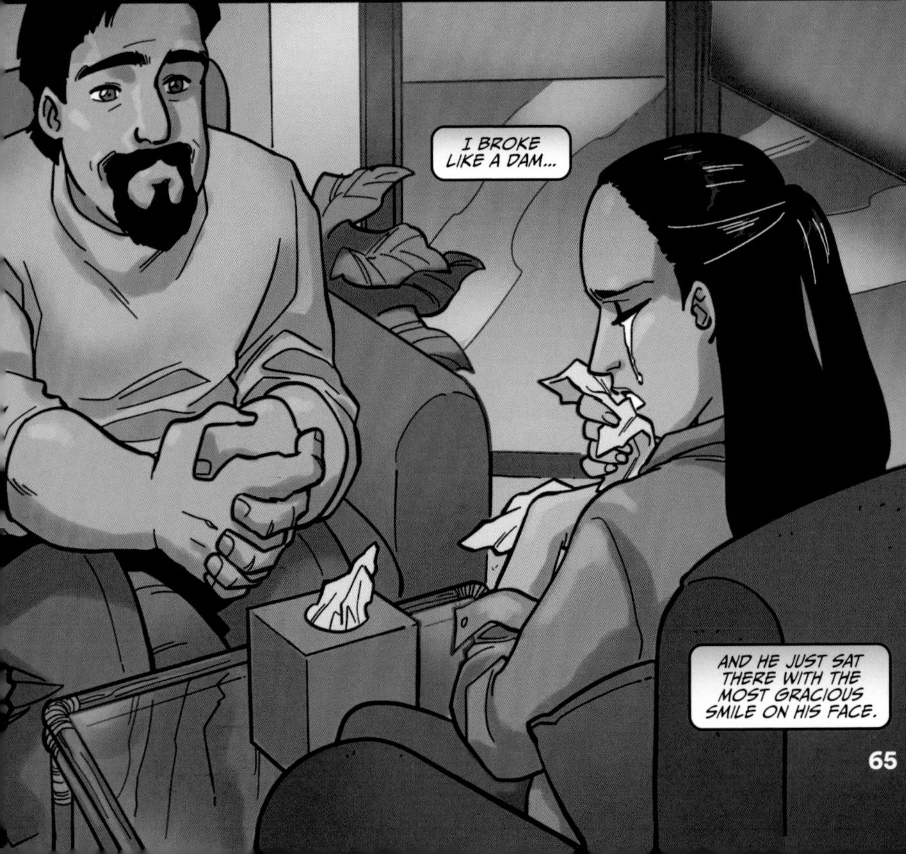
I BROKE LIKE A DAM...
AND HE JUST SAT THERE WITH THE MOST GRACIOUS SMILE ON HIS FACE.

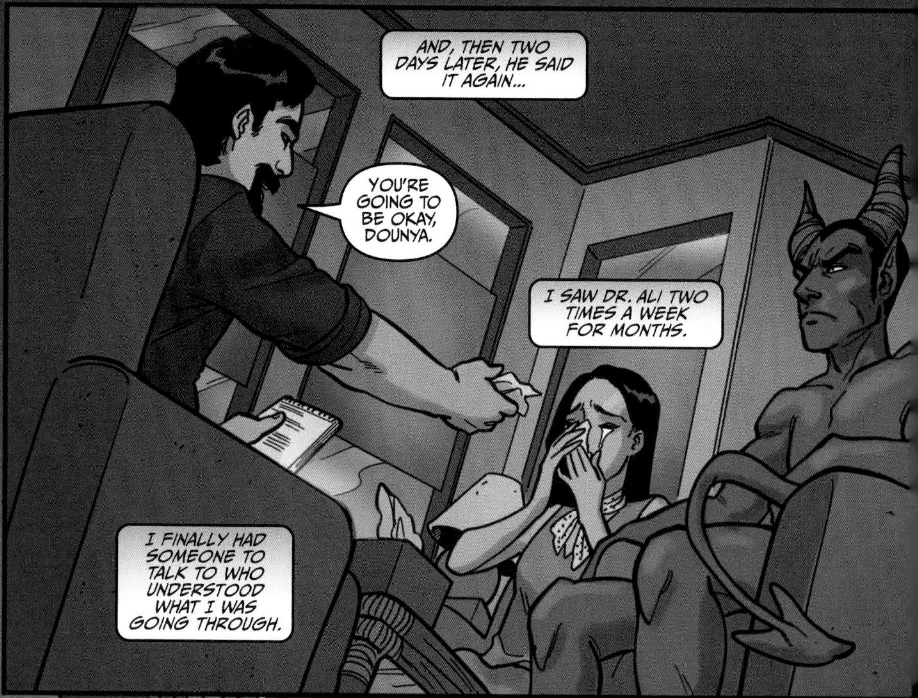
AND, THEN TWO DAYS LATER, HE SAID IT AGAIN...
YOU'RE GOING TO BE OKAY, DOUNYA.
I SAW DR. ALI TWO TIMES A WEEK FOR MONTHS.
I FINALLY HAD SOMEONE TO TALK TO WHO UNDERSTOOD WHAT I WAS GOING THROUGH.

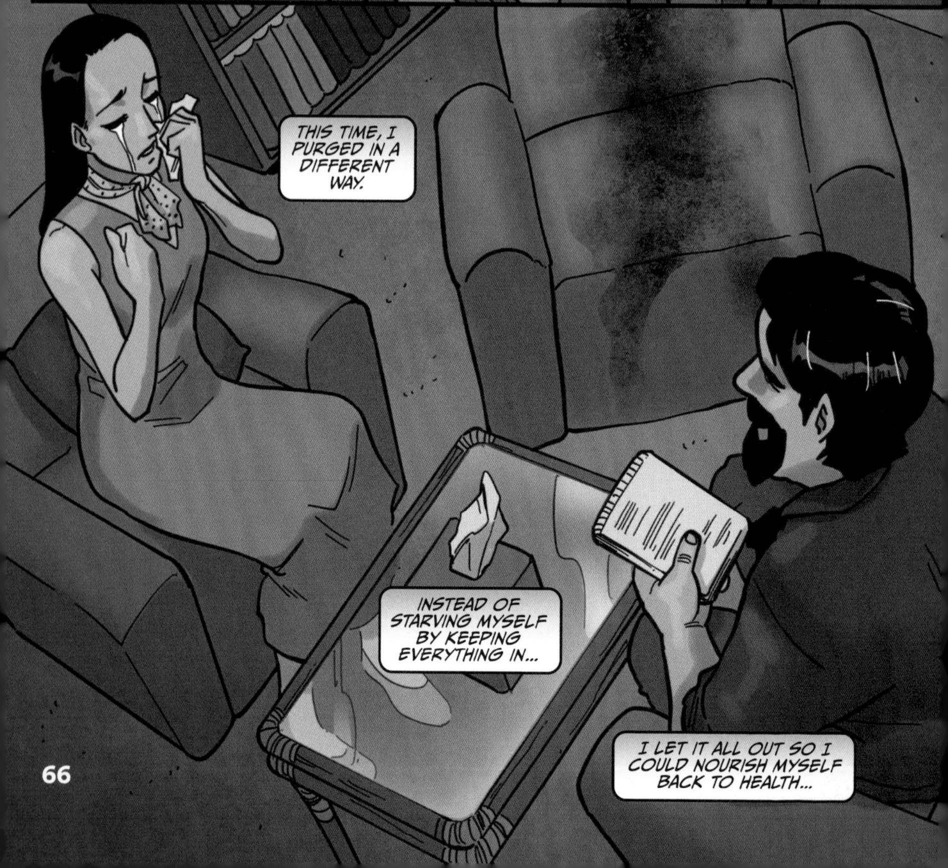
THIS TIME, I PURGED IN A DIFFERENT WAY.
INSTEAD OF STARVING MYSELF BY KEEPING EVERYTHING IN...
I LET IT ALL OUT SO I COULD NOURISH MYSELF BACK TO HEALTH...

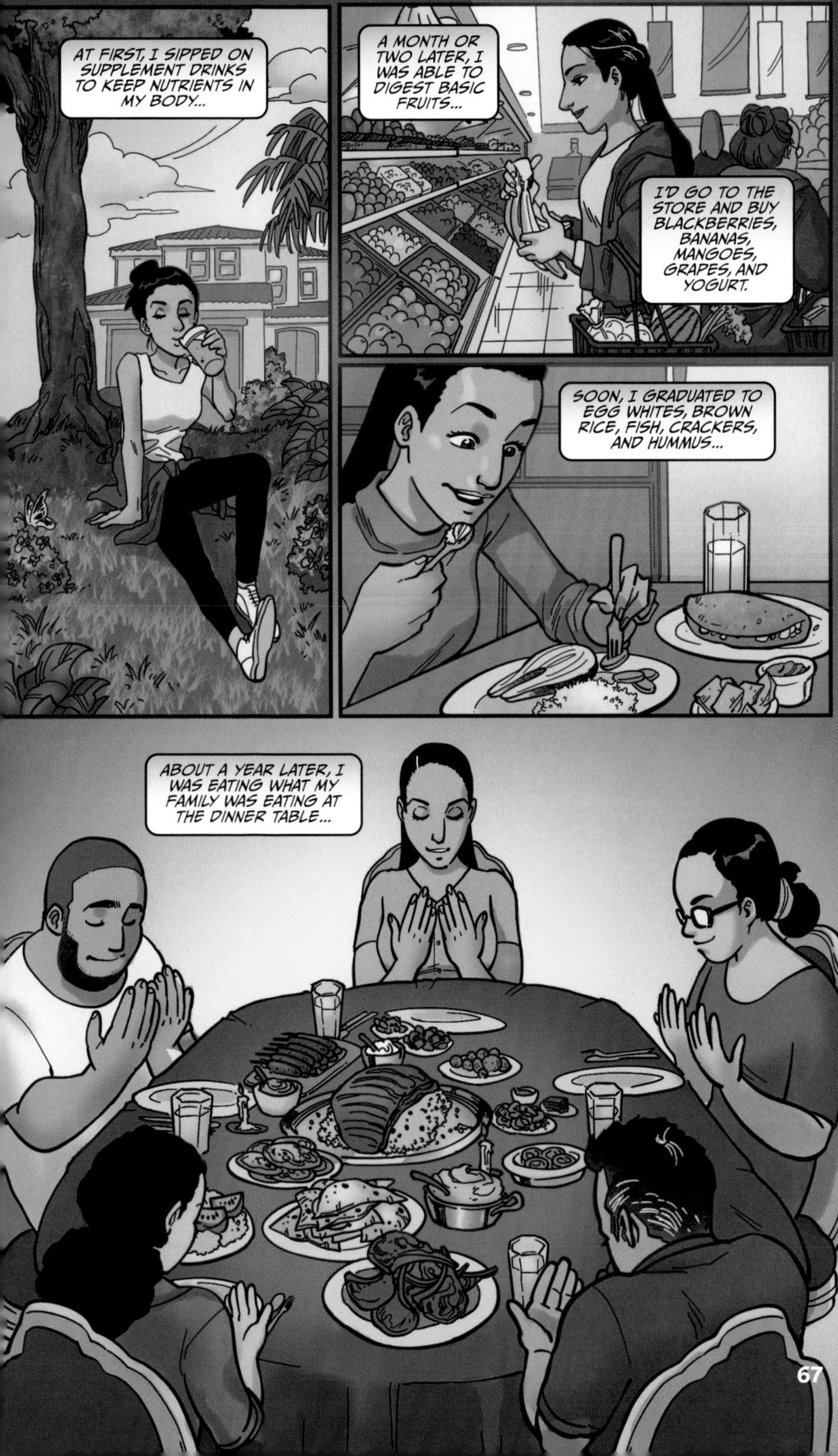
AT FIRST, I SIPPED ON SUPPLEMENT DRINKS TO KEEP NUTRIENTS IN MY BODY...
A MONTH OR TWO LATER, I WAS ABLE TO DIGEST BASIC FRUITS...
I'D GO TO THE STORE AND BUY BLACKBERRIES, BANANAS, MANGOES, GRAPES, AND YOGURT.
SOON, I GRADUATED TO EGG WHITES, BROWN RICE, FISH, CRACKERS, AND HUMMUS...
ABOUT A YEAR LATER, I WAS EATING WHAT MY FAMILY WAS EATING AT THE DINNER TABLE...

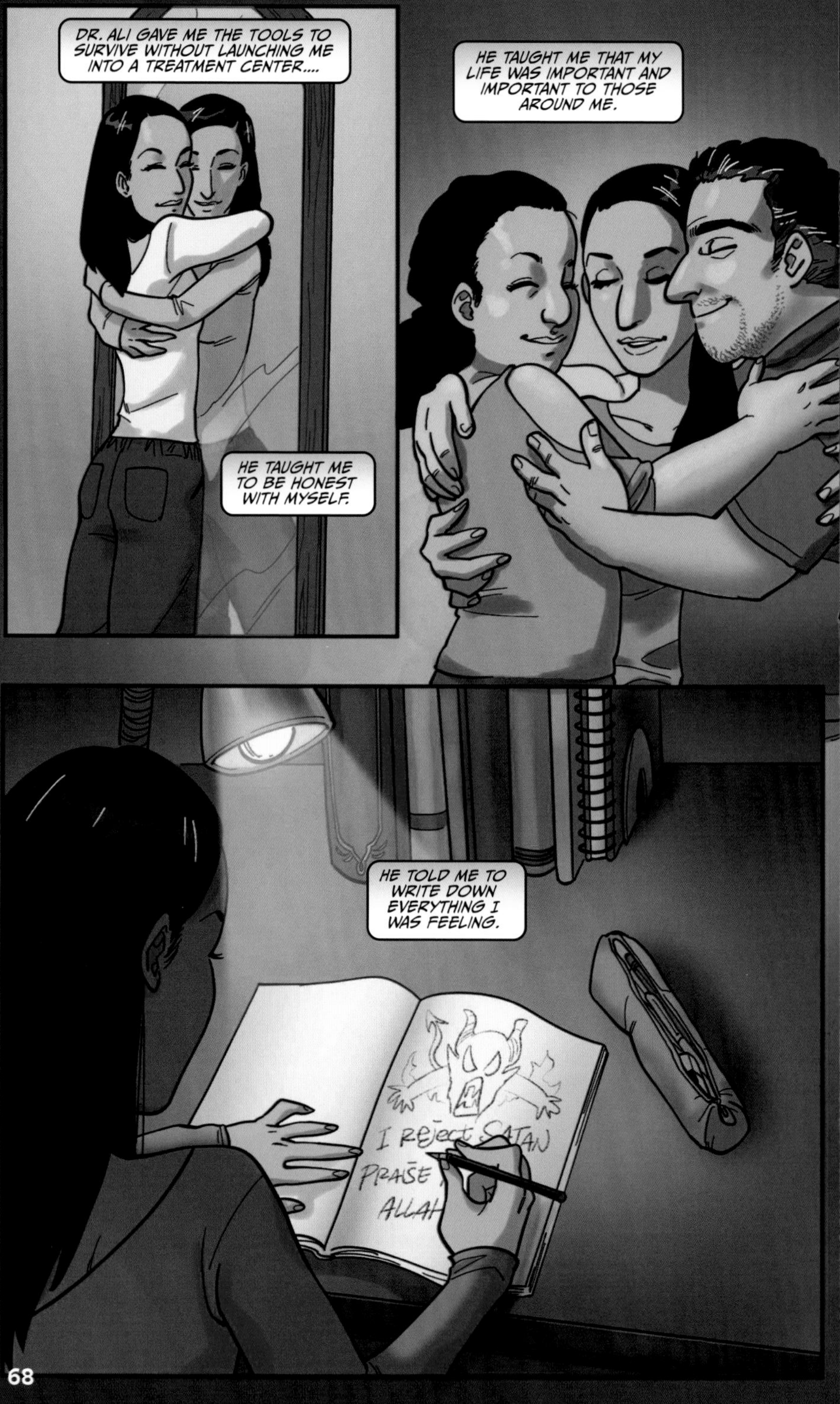
DR. ALI GAVE ME THE TOOLS TO SURVIVE WITHOUT LAUNCHING ME INTO A TREATMENT CENTER....
HE TAUGHT ME TO BE HONEST WITH MYSELF.
HE TAUGHT ME THAT MY LIFE WAS IMPORTANT AND IMPORTANT TO THOSE AROUND ME.
HE TOLD ME TO WRITE DOWN EVERYTHING I WAS FEELING.
I Reject SATAN
PRASE
ALLAH

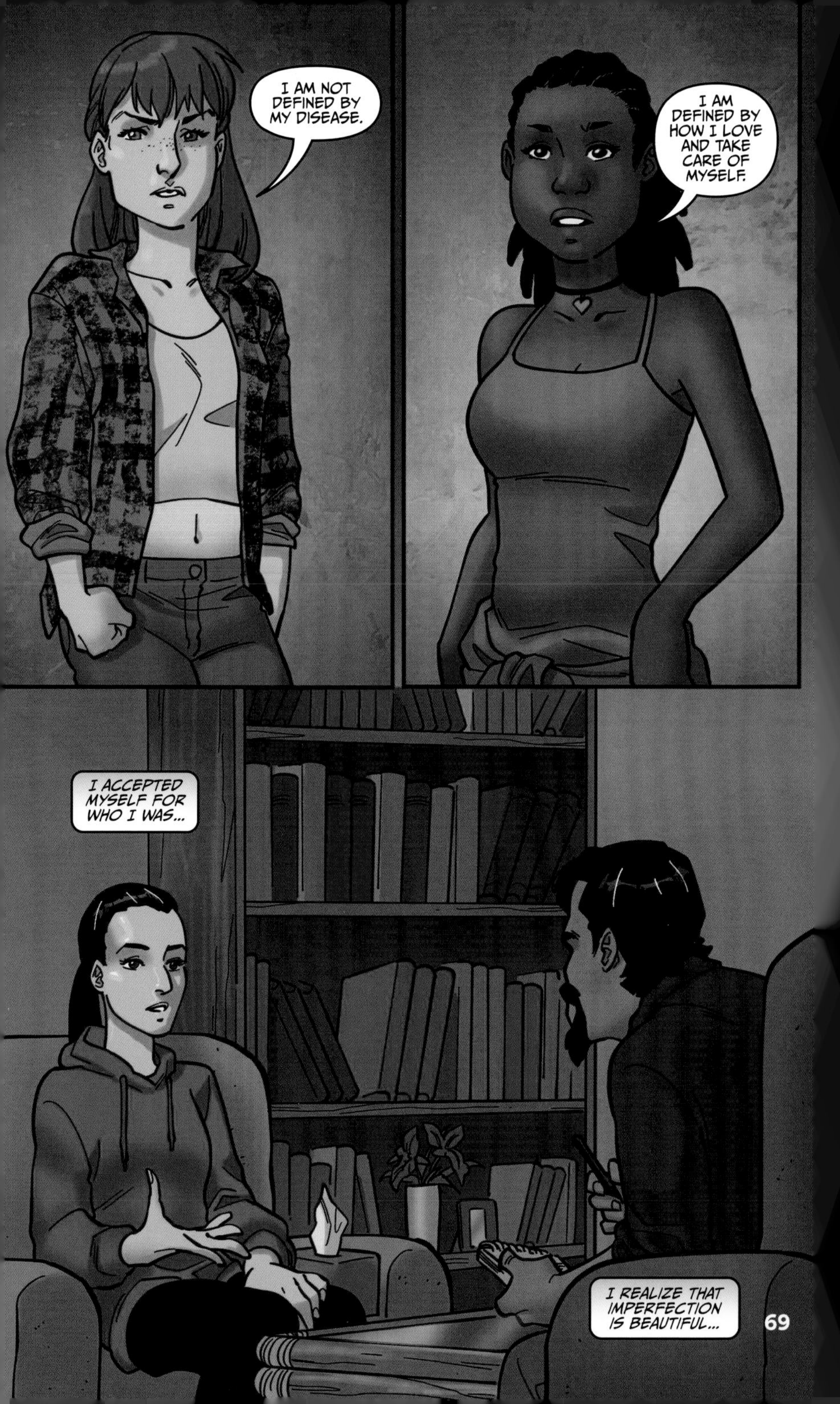
I AM NOT DEFINED BY MY DISEASE.
I AM DEFINED BY HOW I LOVE AND TAKE CARE OF MYSELF.
I ACCEPTED MYSELF FOR WHO I WAS...
I REALIZE THAT IMPERFECTION IS BEAUTIFUL...

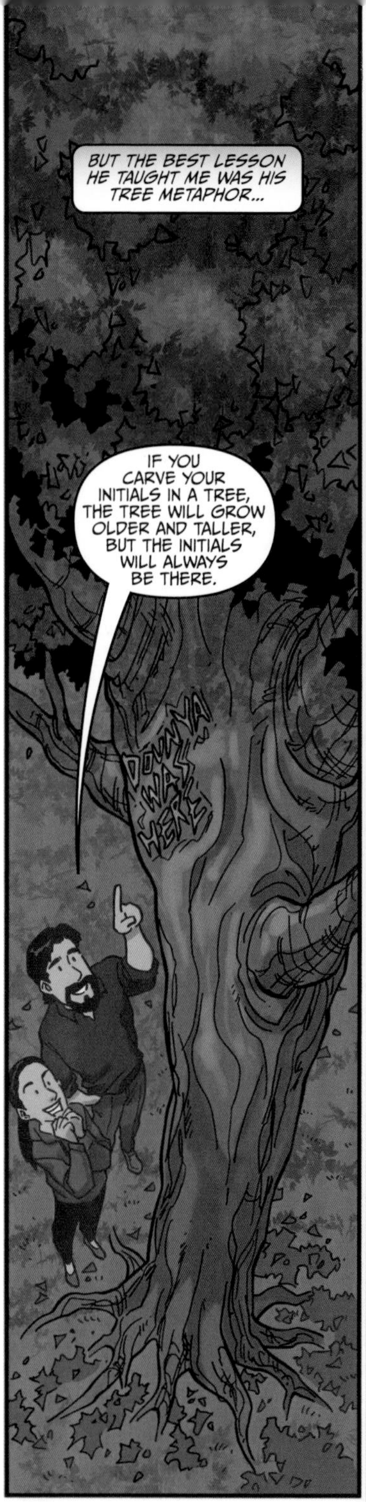
BUT THE BEST LESSON HE TAUGHT ME WAS HIS TREE METAPHOR...
IF YOU CARVE YOUR INITIALS IN A TREE, THE TREE WILL GROW OLDER AND TALLER, BUT THE INITIALS WILL ALWAYS BE THERE.
DONNYA WAS HERE

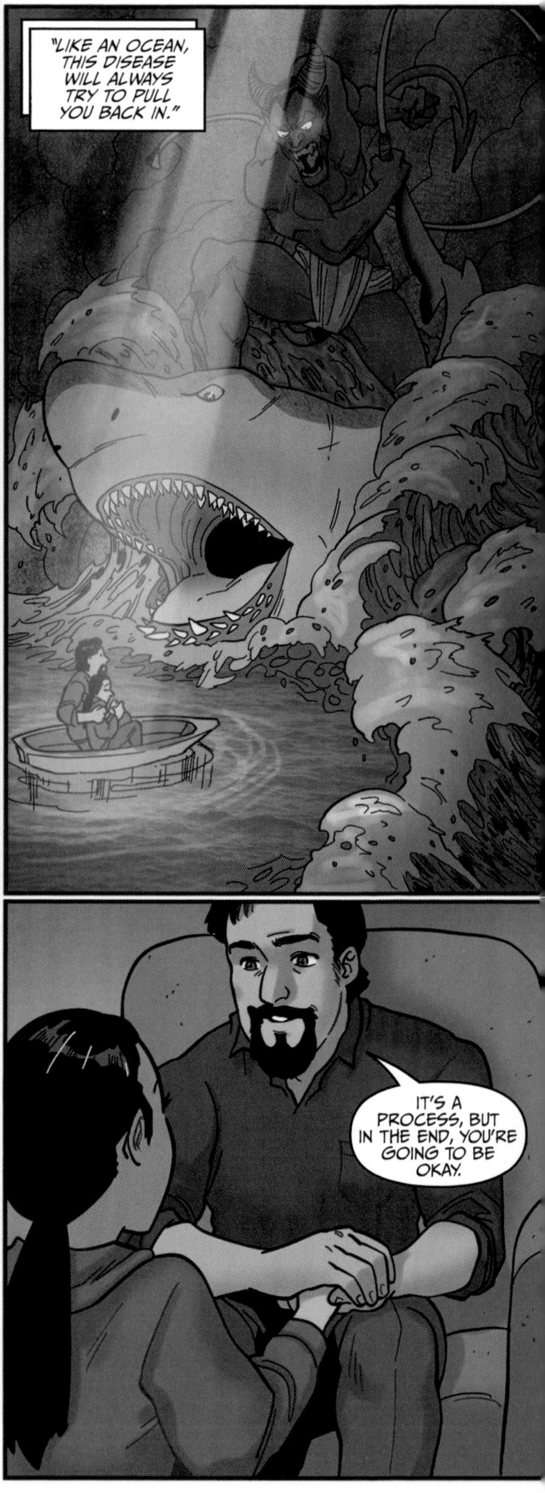
"LIKE AN OCEAN, THIS DISEASE WILL ALWAYS TRY TO PULL YOU BACK IN."
IT'S A PROCESS, BUT IN THE END, YOU'RE GOING TO BE OKAY.

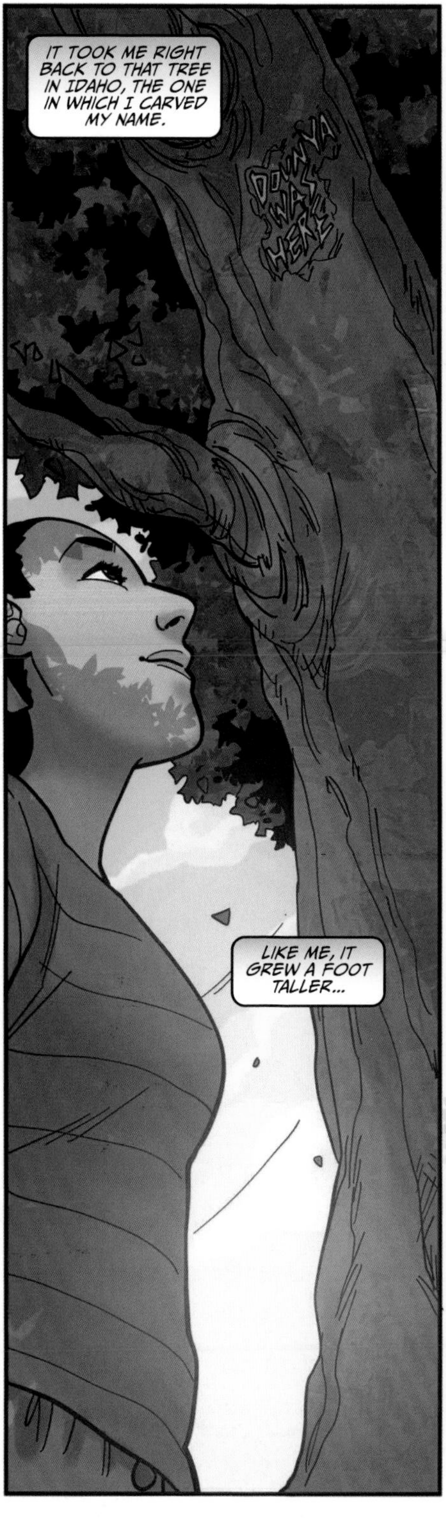
IT TOOK ME RIGHT BACK TO THAT TREE IN IDAHO, THE ONE IN WHICH I CARVED MY NAME.
DOUNYA WAS HERE
LIKE ME, IT GREW A FOOT TALLER...

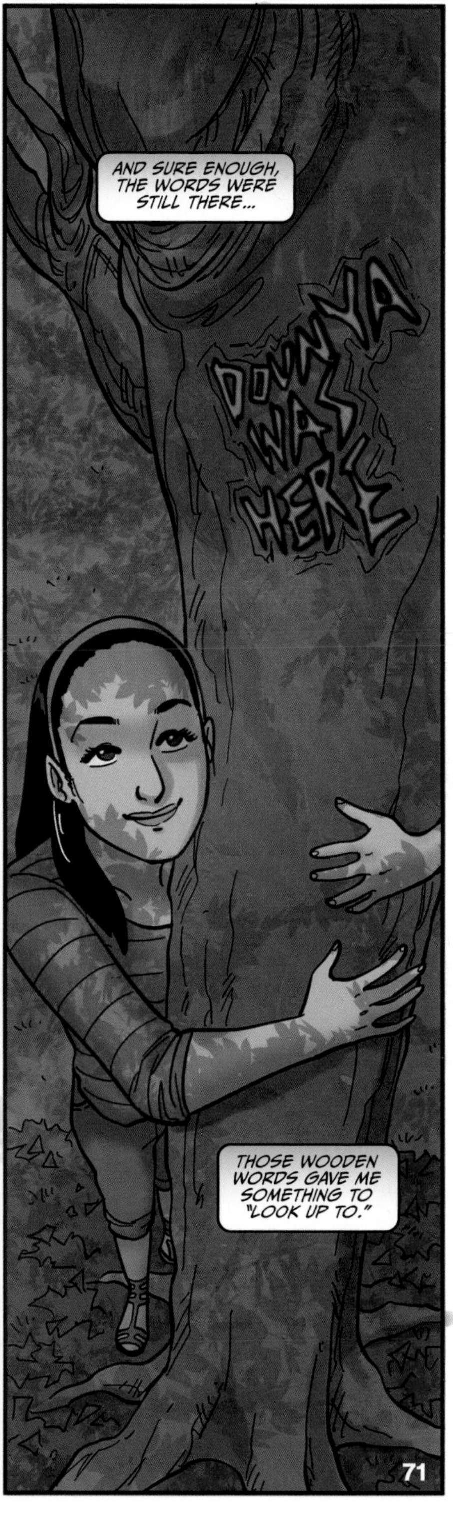
AND SURE ENOUGH, THE WORDS WERE STILL THERE...
DOUNYA WAS HERE
THOSE WOODEN WORDS GAVE ME SOMETHING TO "LOOK UP TO."

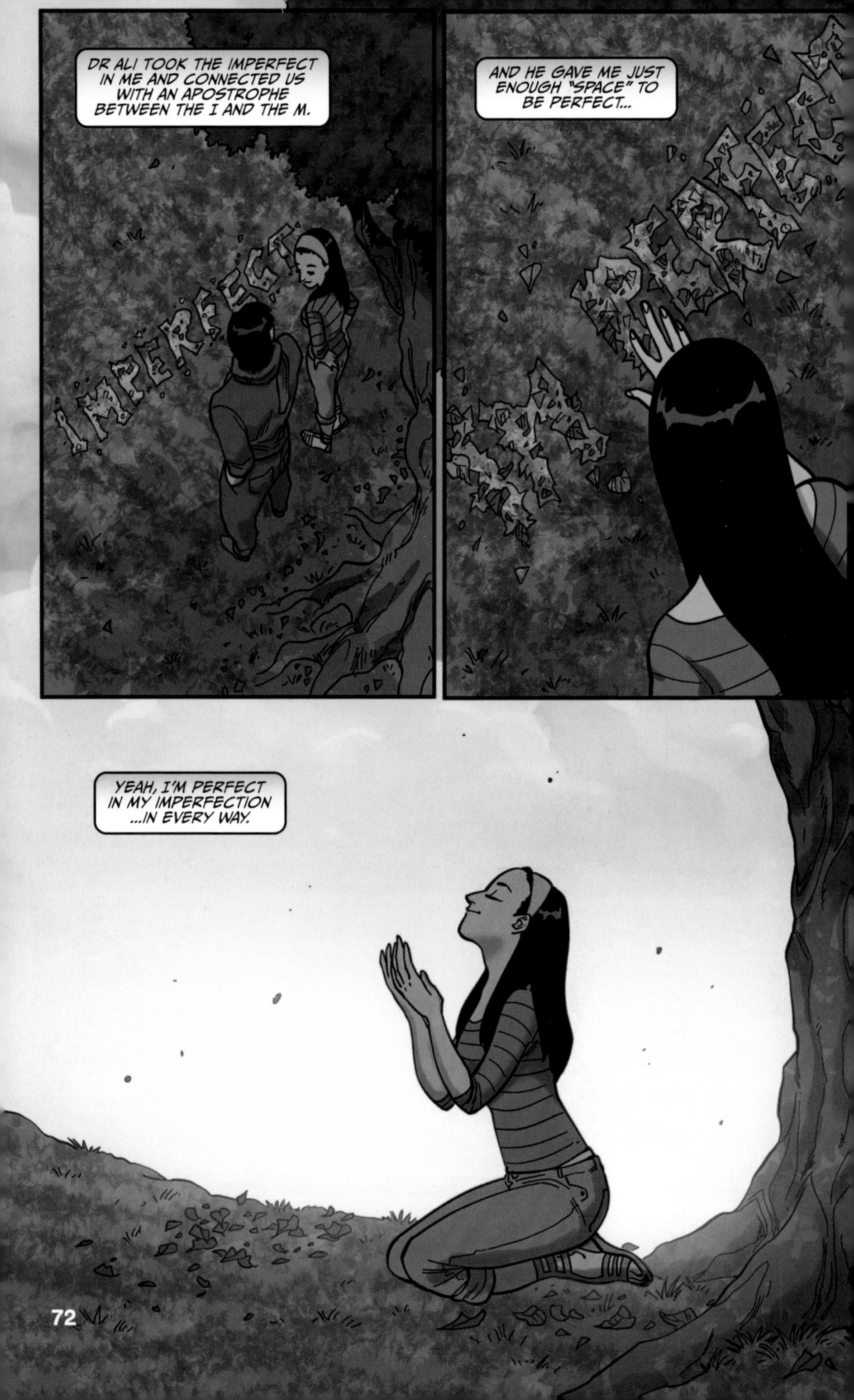
DR ALI TOOK THE IMPERFECT IN ME AND CONNECTED US WITH AN APOSTROPHE BETWEEN THE I AND THE M.
IMPERFECT
AND HE GAVE ME JUST ENOUGH "SPACE" TO BE PERFECT...
YEAH, I'M PERFECT IN MY IMPERFECTION ...IN EVERY WAY.

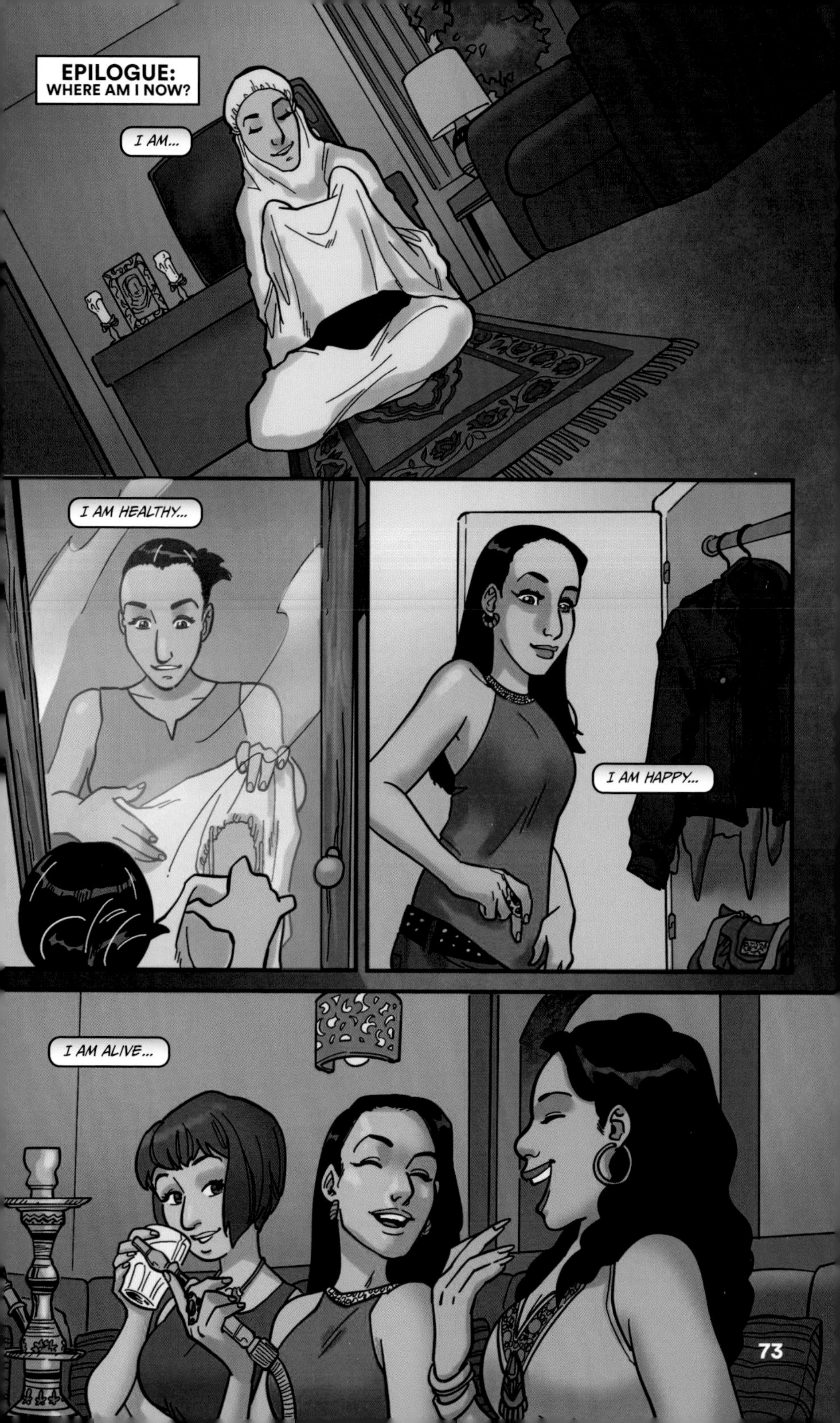
EPILOGUE:
WHERE AM I NOW?
I AM...
I AM HEALTHY...
I AM HAPPY...
I AM ALIVE...

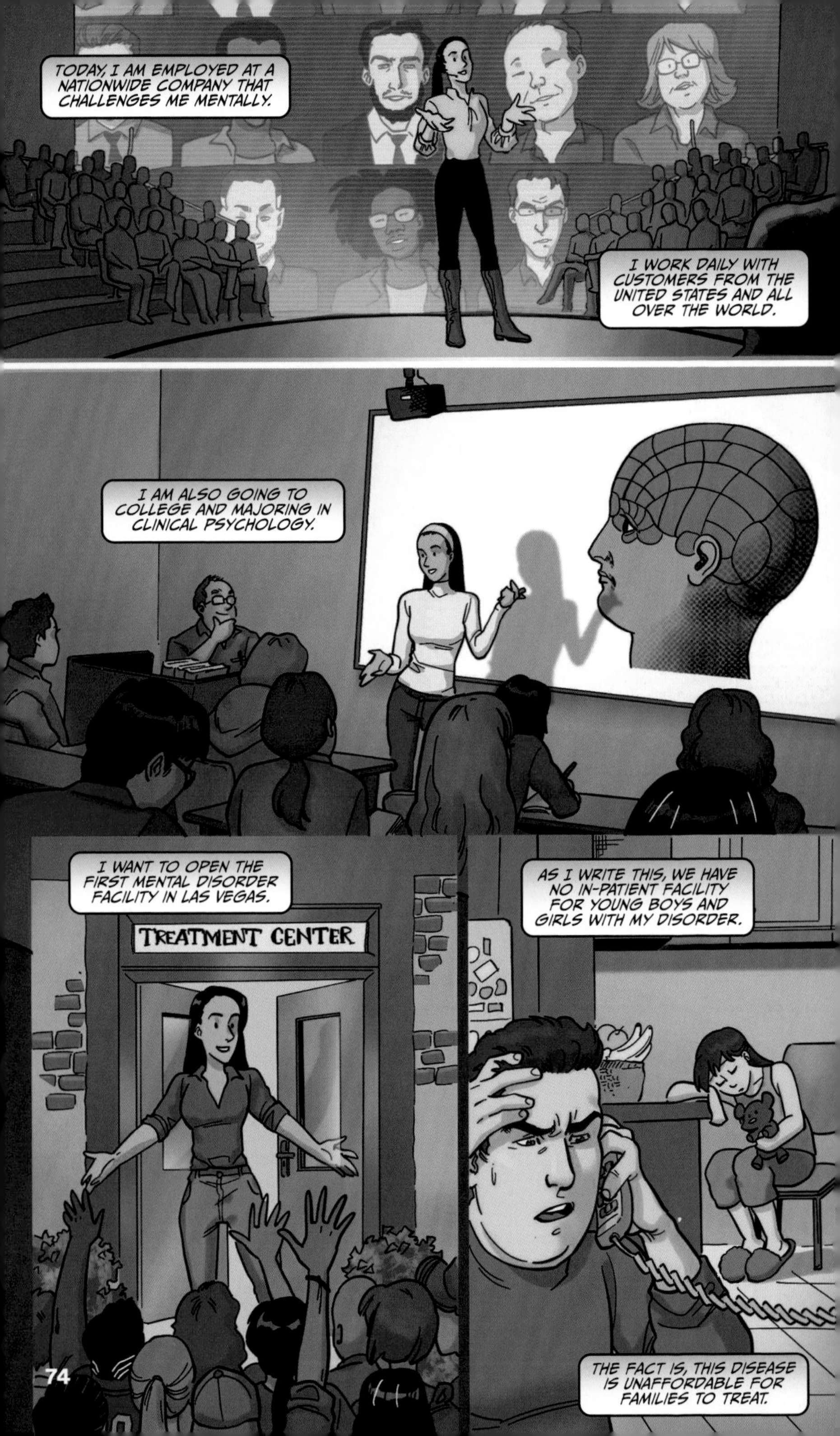
TODAY, I AM EMPLOYED AT A NATIONWIDE COMPANY THAT CHALLENGES ME MENTALLY.
I WORK DAILY WITH CUSTOMERS FROM THE UNITED STATES AND ALL OVER THE WORLD.
I AM ALSO GOING TO COLLEGE AND MAJORING IN CLINICAL PSYCHOLOGY.
I WANT TO OPEN THE FIRST MENTAL DISORDER FACILITY IN LAS VEGAS.
TREATMENT CENTER
AS I WRITE THIS, WE HAVE NO IN-PATIENT FACILITY FOR YOUNG BOYS AND GIRLS WITH MY DISORDER.
THE FACT IS, THIS DISEASE IS UNAFFORDABLE FOR FAMILIES TO TREAT.

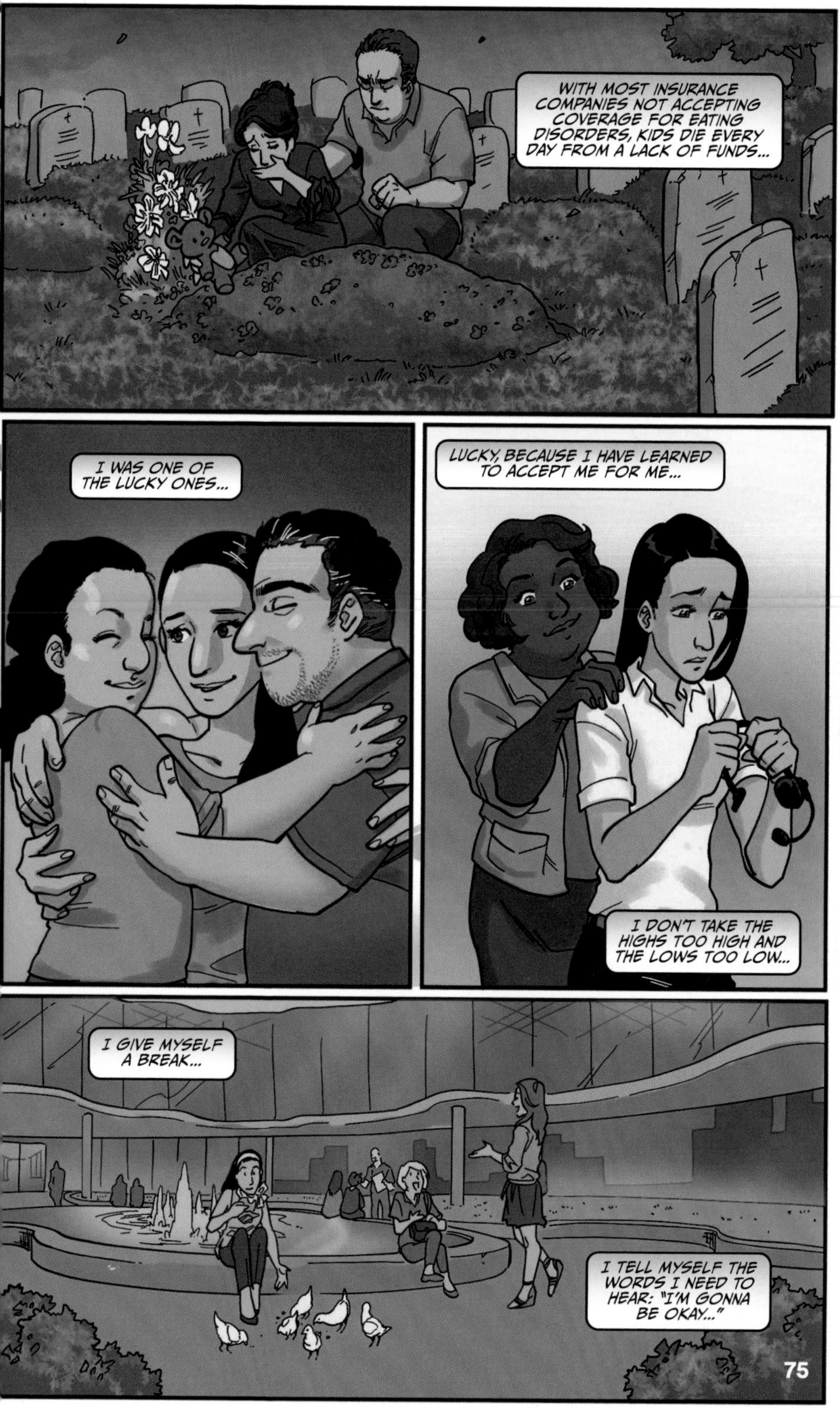
WITH MOST INSURANCE COMPANIES NOT ACCEPTING COVERAGE FOR EATING DISORDERS, KIDS DIE EVERY DAY FROM A LACK OF FUNDS...
I WAS ONE OF THE LUCKY ONES...
LUCKY, BECAUSE I HAVE LEARNED TO ACCEPT ME FOR ME...
I DON'T TAKE THE HIGHS TOO HIGH AND THE LOWS TOO LOW...
I GIVE MYSELF A BREAK...
I TELL MYSELF THE WORDS I NEED TO HEAR: "I'M GONNA BE OKAY..."

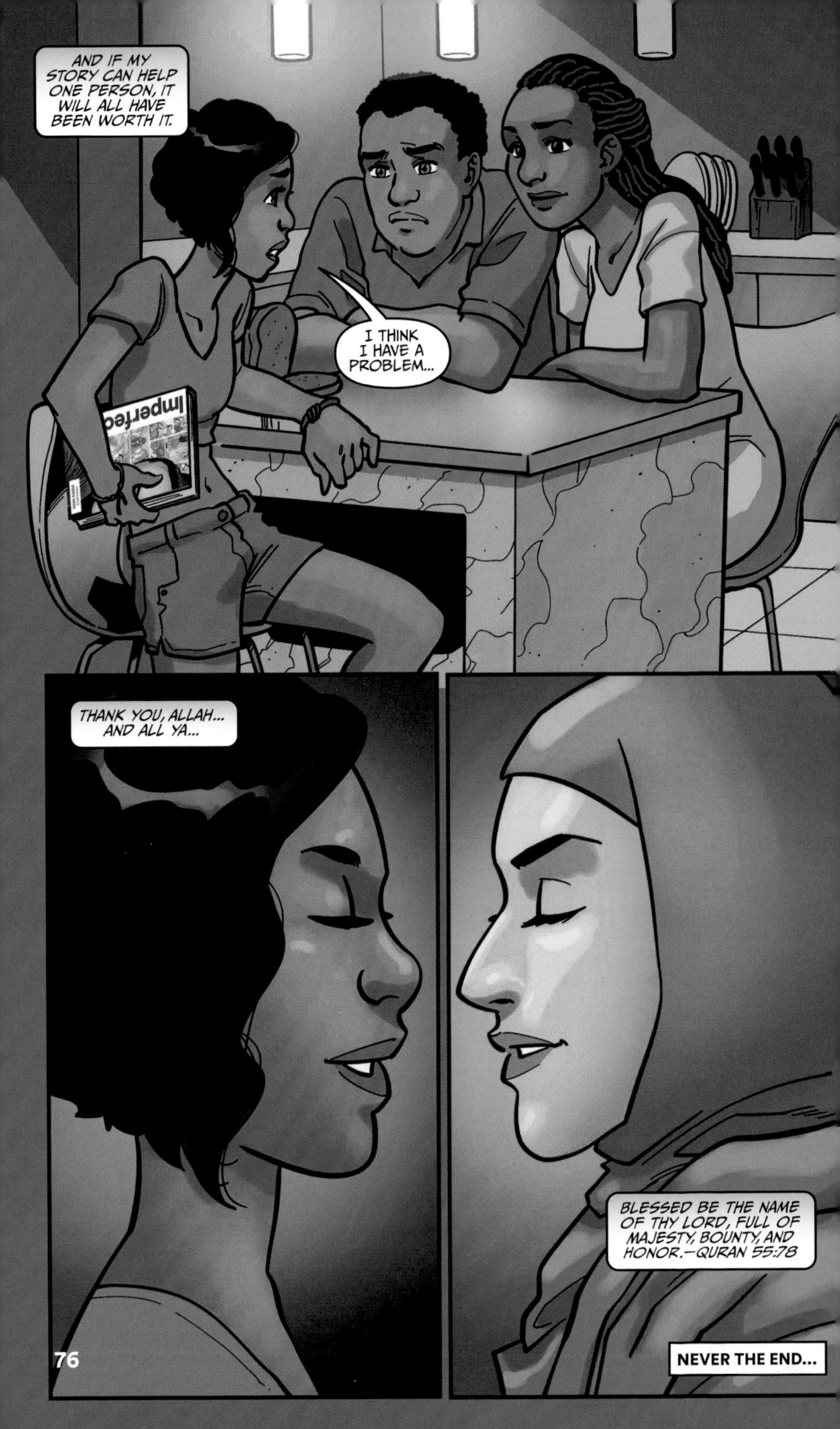
AND IF MY STORY CAN HELP ONE PERSON, IT WILL ALL HAVE BEEN WORTH IT.
I THINK I HAVE A PROBLEM...
THANK YOU, ALLAH... AND ALL YA...
BLESSED BE THE NAME OF THY LORD, FULL OF MAJESTY, BOUNTY, AND HONOR.—QURAN 55:78
NEVER THE END...

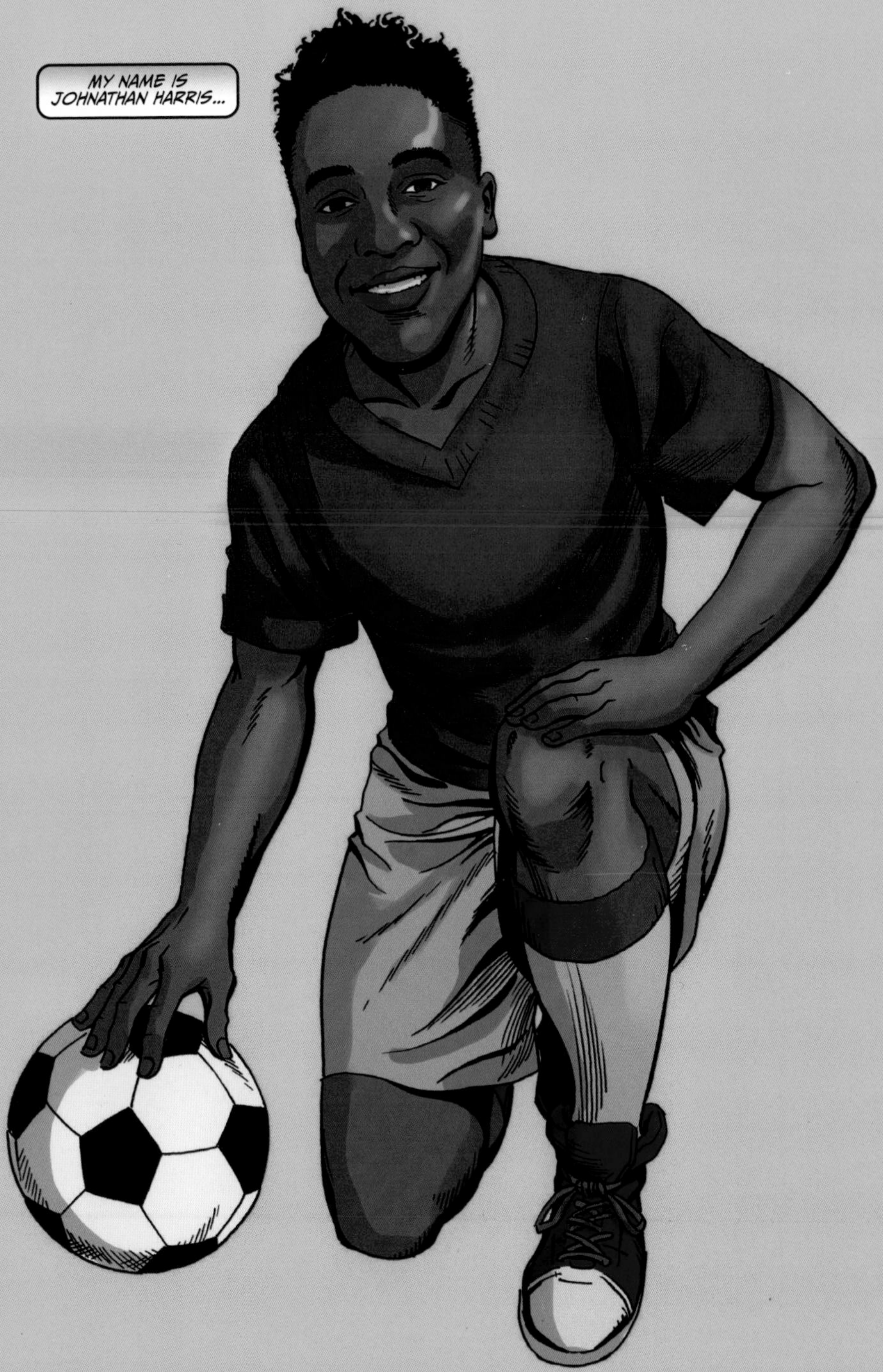
MY NAME IS JOHNATHAN HARRIS...

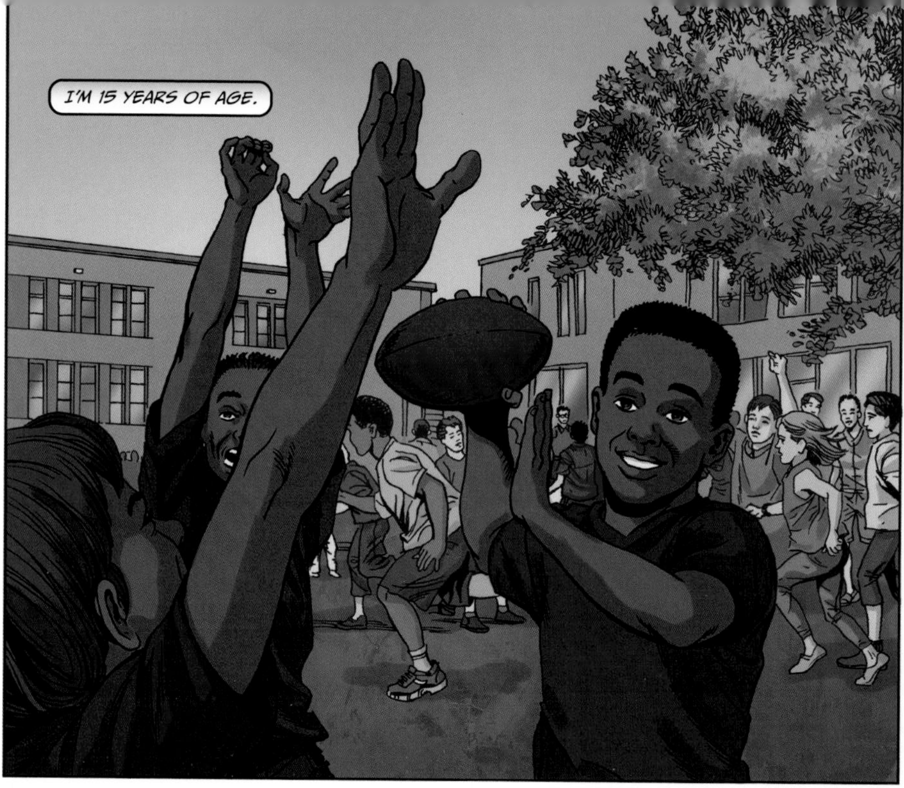
I'M 15 YEARS OF AGE.

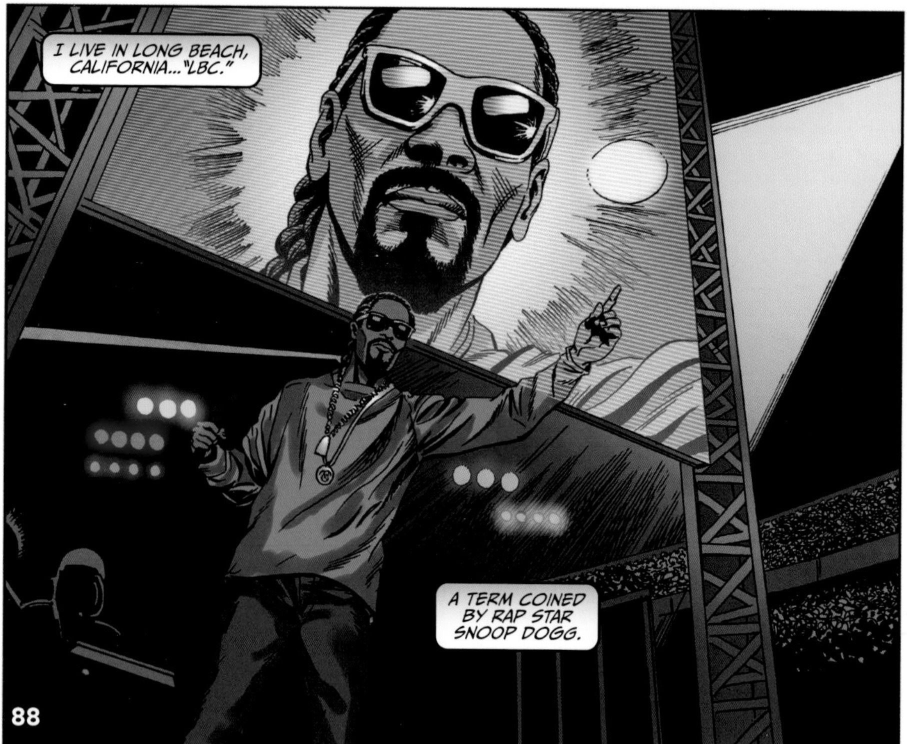
I LIVE IN LONG BEACH, CALIFORNIA..."LBC."
A TERM COINED BY RAP STAR SNOOP DOGG.

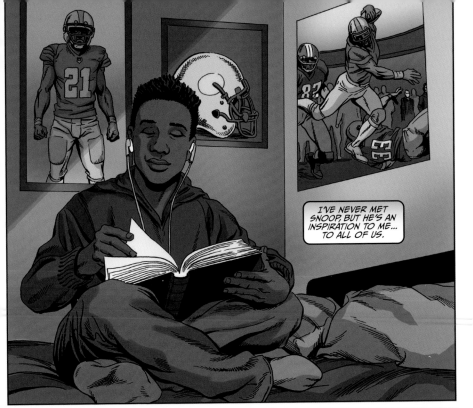

I'VE NEVER MET SNOOP, BUT HE'S AN INSPIRATION TO ME... TO ALL OF US.

HE'S ONE OF THE FEW ARTISTS WHO PUT LONG BEACH ON THE MAP...

AND FOR OUR COMMUNITY, THAT'S A BIG DEAL... ONE OF US MAKING IT...

89

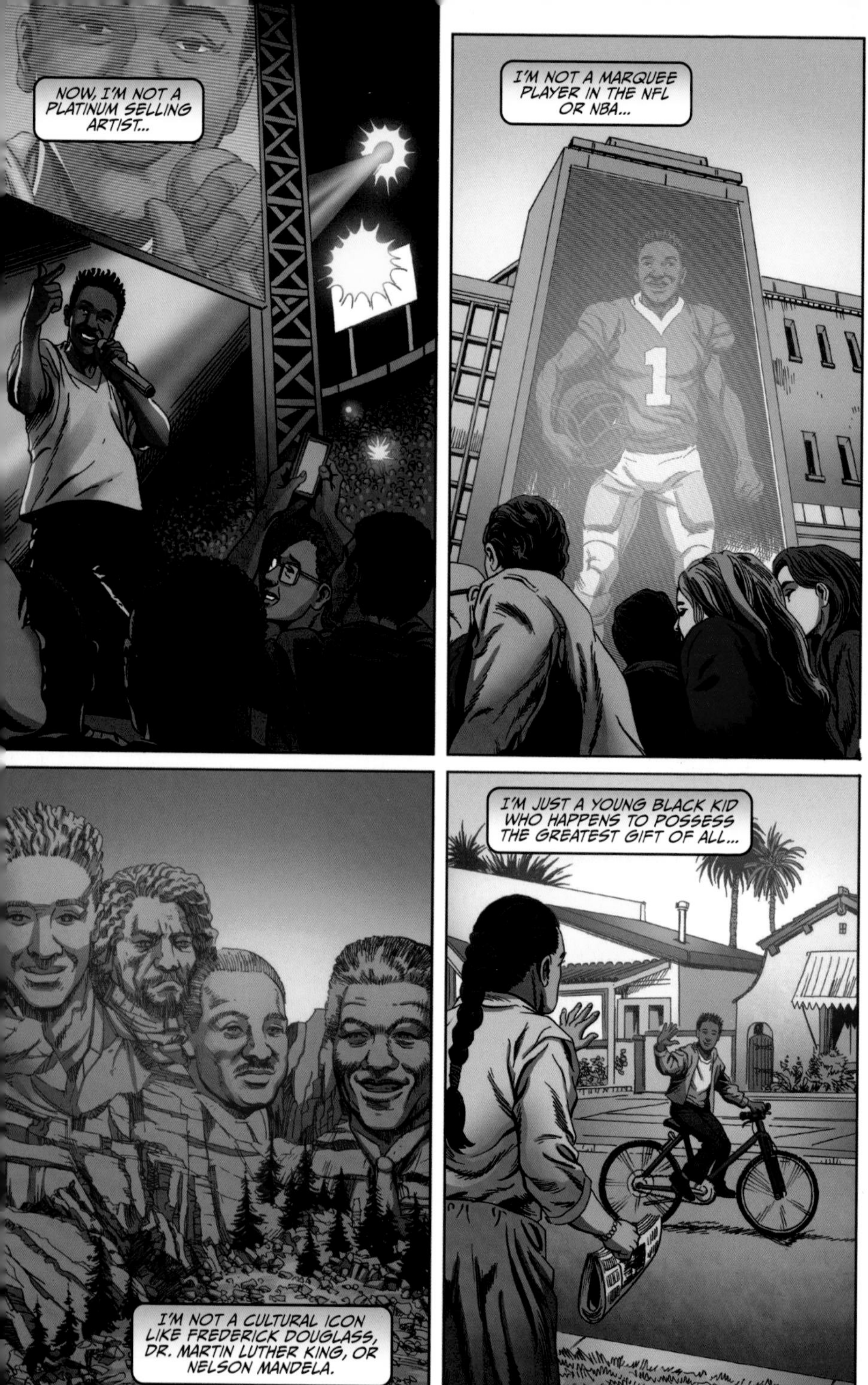
NOW, I'M NOT A PLATINUM SELLING ARTIST...
I'M NOT A MARQUEE PLAYER IN THE NFL OR NBA...
1
I'M NOT A CULTURAL ICON LIKE FREDERICK DOUGLASS, DR. MARTIN LUTHER KING, OR NELSON MANDELA.
I'M JUST A YOUNG BLACK KID WHO HAPPENS TO POSSESS THE GREATEST GIFT OF ALL...

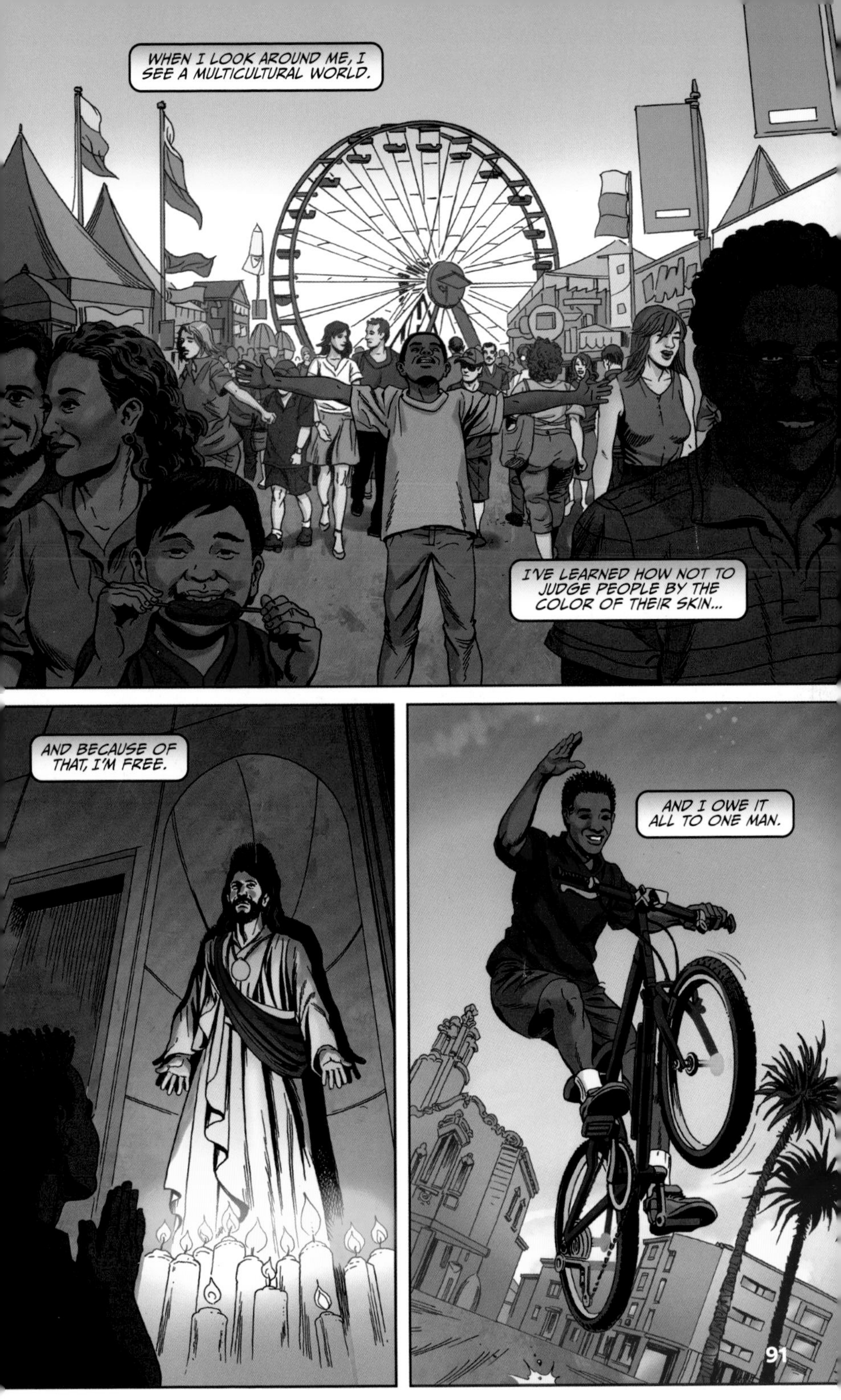
WHEN I LOOK AROUND ME, I SEE A MULTICULTURAL WORLD.
I'VE LEARNED HOW NOT TO JUDGE PEOPLE BY THE COLOR OF THEIR SKIN...
AND BECAUSE OF THAT, I'M FREE.
AND I OWE IT ALL TO ONE MAN.

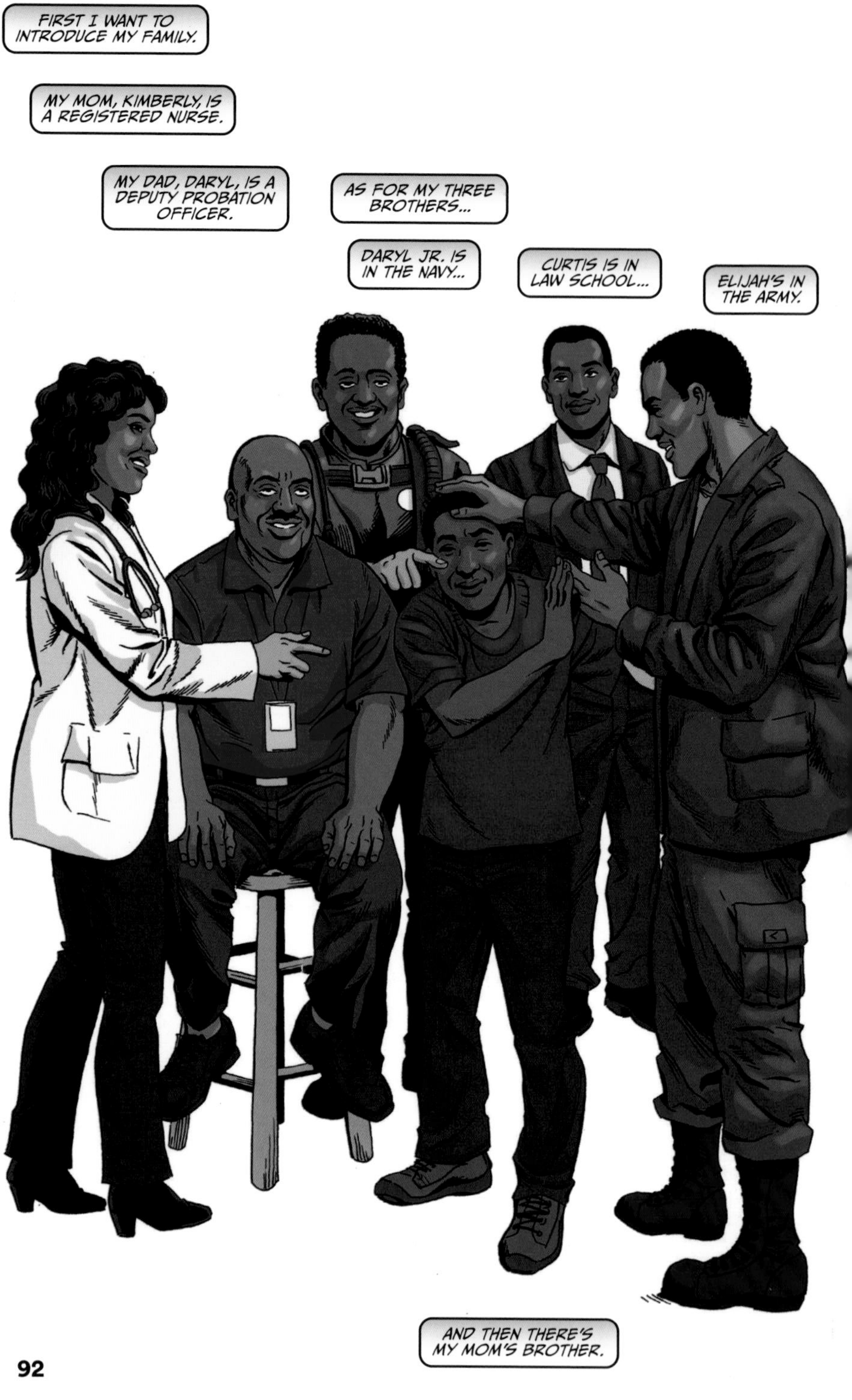
FIRST I WANT TO INTRODUCE MY FAMILY.
MY MOM, KIMBERLY, IS A REGISTERED NURSE.
MY DAD, DARYL, IS A DEPUTY PROBATION OFFICER.
AS FOR MY THREE BROTHERS...
DARYL JR. IS IN THE NAVY...
CURTIS IS IN LAW SCHOOL...
ELIJAH'S IN THE ARMY.
AND THEN THERE'S MY MOM'S BROTHER.

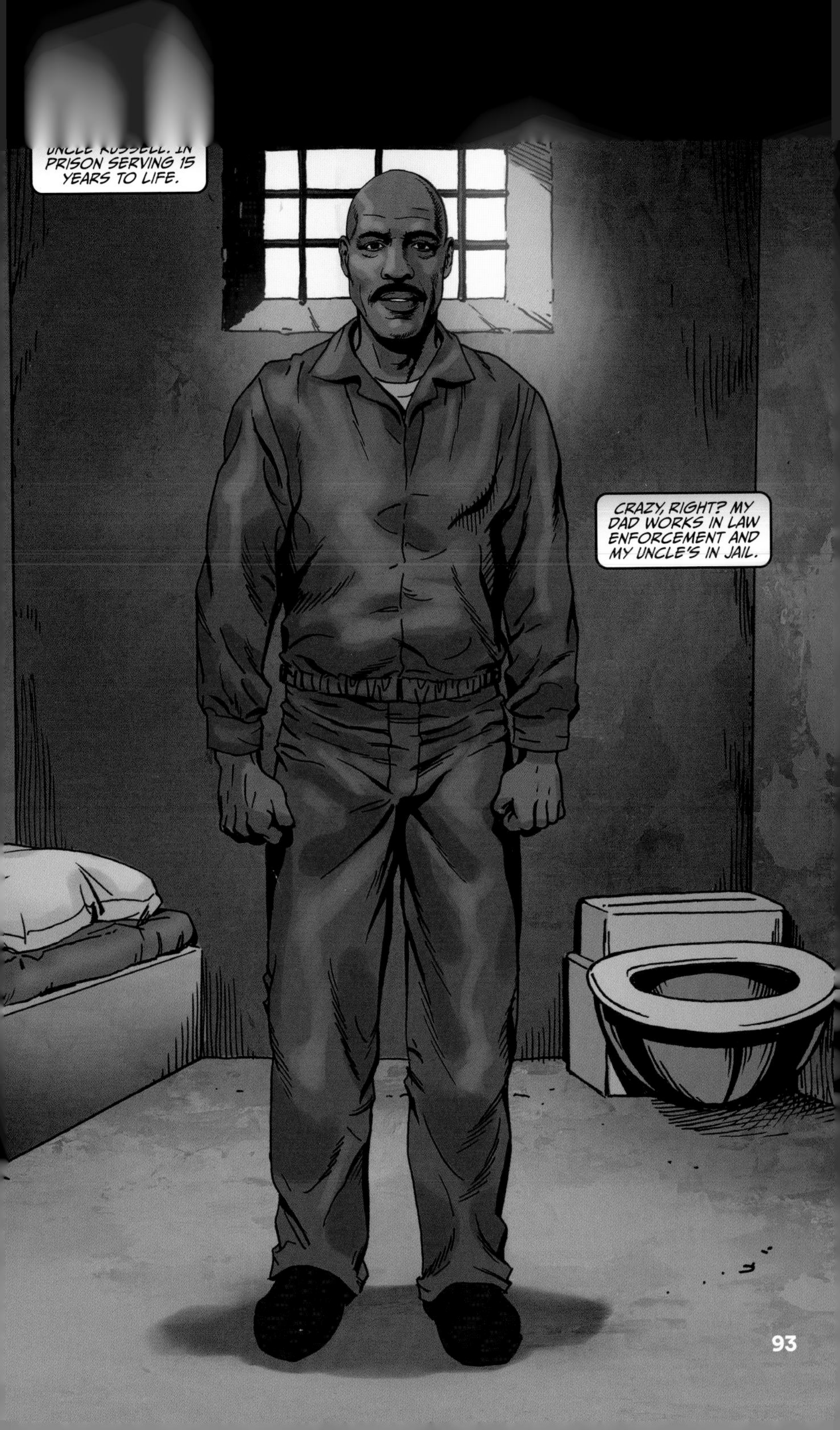
PRISON SERVING 15 YEARS TO LIFE.
CRAZY, RIGHT? MY DAD WORKS IN LAW ENFORCEMENT AND MY UNCLE'S IN JAIL.

TWO OF THE MOST IMPORTANT MEN IN MY LIFE... LIVING TWO COMPLETELY DIFFERENT LIVES.

BUT AS DISTANT AND DIVERSE AS THOSE PATHS ARE...

...ROADS SOMEHOW HAVE A WAY OF CROSSING... FINDING EACH OTHER... AND IN THE END...

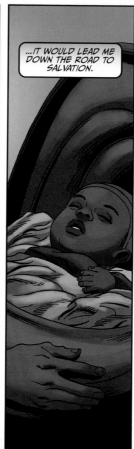

...IT WOULD LEAD ME DOWN THE ROAD TO SALVATION.

THE FIRST TIME I MET MY UNCLE, HE WAS BEHIND BARS.

I WAS JUST SIX MONTHS OLD.

94

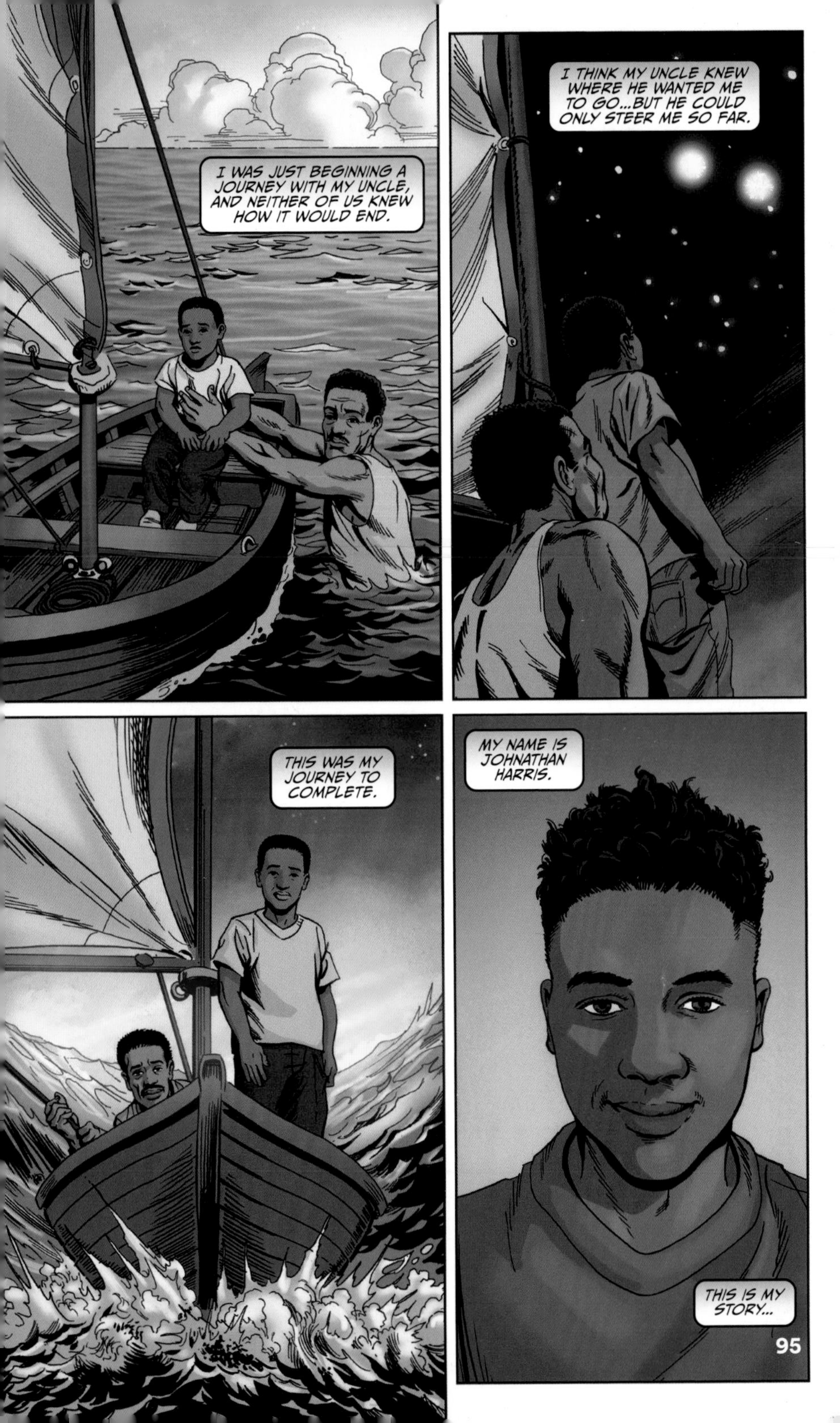

I WAS JUST BEGINNING A JOURNEY WITH MY UNCLE, AND NEITHER OF US KNEW HOW IT WOULD END.
I THINK MY UNCLE KNEW WHERE HE WANTED ME TO GO...BUT HE COULD ONLY STEER ME SO FAR.
THIS WAS MY JOURNEY TO COMPLETE.
MY NAME IS JOHNATHAN HARRIS.
THIS IS MY STORY...

NEW FOR SPRING 2019

Imperfect
A STORY OF BODY IMAGE
A GRAPHIC NOVEL BY
DOUNYA AWADA

IMPERFECT: A STORY OF BODY IMAGE

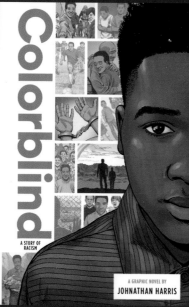

Colorblind
A STORY OF RACISM
A GRAPHIC NOVEL BY
JOHNATHAN HARRIS

COLORBLIND: A STORY OF RACISM

COMING FALL 2019

Activist
A STORY OF THE MARJORY STONEMAN DOUGLAS SHOOTING
A GRAPHIC NOVEL BY
LAUREN HOGG

ACTIVIST: A STORY OF THE MARJORY STONEMAN DOUGLAS SHOOTING

Identity
A STORY OF TRANSITIONING
A GRAPHIC NOVEL BY
COREY MAISON

IDENTITY: A STORY OF TRANSITIONING